Better Homes and Gardens®

Comfort Food

Our seal assures you that every recipe in *Comfort Food* has been tested in the Better Homes and Gardens® Test Kitchen. This means that each recipe is practical and reliable, and meets our high standards of taste appeal. We guarantee your satisfaction with this book for as long as you own it.

WE CARE!

All of us at Better Homes and Gardens® are dedicated to providing you with the information and ideas you need to create tasty foods. We welcome your comments or suggestions. Write to us at: Better Homes and Gardens Books, Cook Book Editorial Department, LS-348, 1716 Locust Street, Des Moines, Iowa 50309-3023

© Copyright 1992 by Meredith Corporation, Des Moines, Iowa. All rights reserved. Printed in the United States of America. First Edition. Printing Number and Year: 5 4 3 2 1   96 95 94 93 92 Library of Congress Catalog Card Number: 90-63303 ISBN: 0-696-01977-9

Sharing favorite foods with family, friends, and neighbors is one of our country's most comforting and memory-making traditions. Through the years, food has remained the focus of many of our activities.

In *Comfort Food,* we celebrate America's love of simple, familiar foods. And we've given these foods new excitement without forgoing their traditional identity. Take a peek at Maple-Nut Cinnamon Rolls and Chicken à la King to see how we've updated many of our treasured treats with tasty new flavor twists.

Cooking for today's life-styles presents some challenges for all of us. That's why we've looked carefully at every recipe, streamlining cooking steps and making each recipe as easy to fix as possible without sacrificing taste. We've even added some recipe variations titled "Make It Easy" for you to use when time is short.

Whatever cozy foods are your favorites, you're sure to enjoy remembering the old and trying the new with *Comfort Food.*

Strawberry Shortcake
(see recipe, page 82)

**Whole Wheat-
Cardamom Rolls**
(see recipe, page 106)

On the front cover: Strawberry Shortcake
(see recipe, page 82)

Contents

Saucy Barbecue Ribs
(see recipe, page 9)
Pasta Salad
(see recipe, page 54)

GREAT MAIN DISHES

*W*ho can resist the permeating aroma of pot roast as it drifts through the kitchen, or the pleasant smoked flavor from a grill? You'll find an abundance of tried and true recipes in this tempting array of entrées. From *Crispy Fried Chicken* to *Beef Stroganoff,* every page overflows with warm, familiar flavors.

Stuffed Pork Chops are pictured at right. (See recipe, page 6.)

Stuffed Pork Chops

Complement tender, juicy pork with a savory corn-bread stuffing featuring hazelnuts and currants. (Pictured on page 5.)

4 pork loin rib chops, cut 1¼ inches thick (about 2 pounds total)

● Trim separable fat from chops. Cut a pocket in each chop by cutting a slit the length of the fat side almost to the bone.

2 cups corn-bread stuffing mix
2 tablespoons margarine *or* butter, melted
¼ cup chopped hazelnuts *or* pecans, toasted
2 tablespoons currants *or* raisins
2 tablespoons thinly sliced green onion
½ cup chicken broth *or* water

● For stuffing, in a mixing bowl combine stuffing mix, margarine or butter, hazelnuts or pecans, currants or raisins, and green onion. Toss with *¼ cup* of the broth or water to moisten. Spoon *2 tablespoons* of the stuffing into *each* pork chop pocket. If necessary, fasten pockets with wooden toothpicks. Stir the remaining broth into the remaining stuffing.

Place stuffed chops on a rack in a shallow roasting pan. Place remaining stuffing in a greased 1-quart casserole and refrigerate till ready to bake.

⅓ cup currant *or* crab apple jelly
1 tablespoon lemon juice *or* white wine vinegar
½ teaspoon ground ginger

● For the glaze, in a small saucepan cook and stir jelly, lemon juice or vinegar, and ginger till jelly is melted. Brush chops with some of the glaze.

● Bake chops, uncovered, in a 375° oven for 25 minutes. Brush again with glaze. Place casserole of stuffing in oven beside the pork chops. Bake about 15 minutes or till no pink remains and stuffing is heated through. Makes 4 servings.

Nutrition information per serving: 564 calories, 35 g protein, 44 g carbohydrate, 27 g fat (7 g saturated), 103 mg cholesterol, 571 mg sodium, 555 mg potassium.

Grill Directions: Prepare Stuffed Pork Chops as above, *except* tear off an 18x24-inch piece of heavy-duty foil. Fold in half to make a double thickness of foil that measures 12x18 inches. Place remaining stuffing in the center of foil. Bring up long edges of foil and seal with a double fold. Then fold short ends to completely encase the stuffing, leaving space for steam to build. Refrigerate packet till ready to grill.

In a covered grill arrange preheated coals around a drip pan. Test for *medium* heat above the pan. (See tip, page 35.) Place chops on the grill rack over the drip pan but not over the coals. Lower grill hood. Grill for 15 minutes. Brush with glaze; turn chops. Brush again.

Place foil packet of stuffing on grill rack beside chops. Grill 15 to 20 minutes more or till no pink remains. Brush with glaze.

Roast Pork with Curry Sauce

Enjoy this robust curry sauce with broiled or grilled chicken, too.

1 1½- to 2-pound boneless pork top
   loin roast (single)
¼ teaspoon salt
¼ teaspoon pepper

● Rub roast with salt and pepper. Place roast on a rack in a shallow roasting pan. Insert meat thermometer. Roast in a 325° oven for 1 to 1¼ hours or till meat thermometer registers 160°. Transfer meat to a serving platter. Keep warm.

¼ cup sliced green onion
1 clove garlic, minced
1 tablespoon margarine *or* butter
2 teaspoons curry powder
4 teaspoons all-purpose flour
   Dash salt
¼ cup plain yogurt *or* dairy sour cream
¾ cup milk
¼ cup raisins
   Chopped peanuts (optional)

● For the sauce, in a small saucepan cook onion and garlic in margarine or butter till onion is tender. Stir in curry powder and cook for 1 minute more. Stir flour and salt into yogurt or sour cream. Gradually stir milk into yogurt mixture. Stir yogurt mixture and raisins into the onion mixture in the saucepan.

   Cook and stir sauce till thickened and bubbly. Cook and stir 1 minute more. Pass curry sauce with roast. If desired, serve with chopped peanuts. Makes 6 to 8 servings.

Nutrition information per serving: 273 calories, 25 g protein, 10 g carbohydrate, 15 g fat (5 g saturated), 80 mg cholesterol, 215 mg sodium, 461 mg potassium.

Pork Update

Today's pork is leaner and lower in fat and calories than ever before. And because there is so little fat in today's pork, it is essential to not overcook pork to ensure the most flavorful, tender, and juicy meat.

   To achieve the best flavor, the latest pork cookery recommendations now offer you a choice of doneness with selected pork cuts. Selected cuts such as boneless or bone-in loin can be cooked to medium (160°F) or to well done (170°).

   Use these guidelines for doneness when you cook pork. When boneless pork is cooked to medium or 160°F, the meat will be faintly pink in the center; at 170°F, the meat loses its pink color. Bone-in cuts will have a slightly more intense pink color near the bone when cooked to 160°F, but are perfectly safe to eat.

BACKYARD BARBECUE

*F*ire up the grill, clean off the picnic table, and invite family, friends, and neighbors in for a fun and memorable event.

MENU

●

SAUCY BARBECUE RIBS
(page 9)

PASTA SALAD
(page 54)

CORN ON THE COB

APPLE PIE WITH CIDER SAUCE
(page 93)

Menu Countdown

1 Day Ahead: Boil and refrigerate ribs. Prepare and refrigerate the sauce for *Saucy Barbecue Ribs*. Prepare and refrigerate the *Pasta Salad*.
8 Hours Ahead: Prepare *Apple Pie with Cider Sauce*.

1¼ Hours Ahead: Start coals.
1 Hour Ahead: Prepare the Cider Sauce for *Apple Pie with Cider Sauce*.
45 Minutes Ahead: Grill the *Saucy Barbecue Ribs*.
5 Minutes Ahead: Toss tomatoes with the *Pasta Salad*.

Saucy Barbecue Ribs

Simmer the sauce and the ribs the day before you plan to serve them. Then cover and chill the ribs for an easy-to-fix meal the next day.

2½ to 3 pounds pork loin back ribs *or* meaty pork spareribs

● Cut ribs into serving-size pieces. Place ribs in a Dutch oven. Add enough water to cover the ribs. Bring to boiling; reduce heat. Cover and simmer for 30 minutes. Drain.

⅓ cup chopped onion
1 clove garlic, minced
1 tablespoon cooking oil
½ cup red currant jelly
½ cup chili sauce
2 tablespoons Worcestershire sauce
1 tablespoon vinegar
¼ teaspoon celery seed

● Meanwhile, for sauce, in a small saucepan cook the onion and garlic in hot oil till onion is tender. Stir in the jelly, chili sauce, Worcestershire sauce, vinegar, and celery seed. Bring mixture to boiling; reduce heat. Simmer, uncovered, for 5 to 10 minutes or to desired consistency, stirring occasionally.

● In a covered grill arrange preheated coals around a drip pan. Test for *slow* heat above pan. (See tip, page 35.) Pour 1 inch of water into pan. Place ribs on the grill rack over drip pan, but not over coals. Lower grill hood. Grill about 45 minutes or till tender, occasionally brushing with sauce. Pass any remaining sauce with ribs. Makes 4 servings.

Nutrition information per serving: 395 calories, 26 g protein, 37 g carbohydrate, 16 g fat (5 g saturated), 70 mg cholesterol, 589 mg sodium, 562 mg potassium.

Oven Directions: Prepare Saucy Barbecue Ribs as above, *except* omit boiling and grilling. If desired, cut ribs into serving-size pieces. Place ribs, bone side down, on a rack in a shallow roasting pan. Roast in a 350° oven for 1 hour. Drain off fat. Spoon some of the sauce over ribs. Roast ribs, loosely covered with foil, for 30 to 60 minutes more or till well-done, occasionally spooning sauce over ribs. Serve as above.

Ham with Cranberry-Plum Sauce

1 2- to 2½-pound boneless fully cooked ham portion *or* one 2-pound fully cooked center-cut ham slice, cut 1 inch thick

● If using ham portion, place on a rack in a shallow baking pan. If desired, score the top in a diamond pattern. Insert a meat thermometer. Roast in a 325° oven for 1 to 1½ hours or till thermometer registers 140°. Slice to serve.

  If using ham slice, trim separable fat from ham slice. Slash edges at 1-inch intervals. Place on a rack in a shallow baking pan. Bake in a 350° oven for 30 to 40 minutes or till heated through.

1 cup cranberries
½ cup water

● Meanwhile, for sauce, in a medium saucepan combine cranberries and water. Bring to boiling; reduce heat. Simmer, covered, for 3 to 4 minutes or till skins pop. Drain.

½ cup plum preserves
2 tablespoons sliced green onion
1 teaspoon Worcestershire sauce
¼ teaspoon crushed red pepper (optional)

● In the saucepan combine cranberries, plum preserves, green onion, Worcestershire sauce, and, if desired, crushed red pepper. Heat over low heat till preserves are melted and mixture is hot. Serve sauce with ham. Serves 8 to 10.

Nutrition information per serving: 216 calories, 25 g protein, 16 g carbohydrate, 6 g fat (2 g saturated), 55 mg cholesterol, 1,326 mg sodium, 345 mg potassium.

Cheesy Bratwurst and Cabbage

4 fully cooked smoked bratwurst, knockwurst, *or* Polish sausage

● Make slits in bratwurst, knockwurst, or Polish sausage at 1-inch intervals, cutting to, *but not through,* the opposite side. Set aside.

6 cups shredded cabbage
1 cup water
½ cup chopped onion
½ cup shredded carrot
1 teaspoon caraway seed
¼ teaspoon pepper
⅛ teaspoon salt

● In a 12-inch skillet combine cabbage, water, onion, carrot, caraway, pepper, and salt. Arrange bratwurst atop. Bring to boiling; reduce heat. Cover and simmer for 10 to 15 minutes or till cabbage is tender and bratwurst is heated through.

4 ounces process Swiss cheese, torn

● Remove bratwurst from skillet; keep warm. Drain cabbage mixture. Add Swiss cheese to cabbage. Stir over low heat till cheese is melted. Serve cabbage with bratwurst. Serves 4.

Nutrition information per serving: 344 calories, 17 g protein, 11 g carbohydrate, 26 g fat (12 g saturated), 63 mg cholesterol, 1,164 mg sodium, 540 mg potassium.

Corn Dogs

Introduced at a ball game in the early 1900s, frankfurters are synonymous with American celebrations. Corn Dogs are a popular variation of the festive frank, which was dubbed "hot dog" shortly after its debut.

1 pound frankfurters (8 to 10)

● Pat frankfurters dry with paper towels. If desired, insert a sturdy wooden skewer into 1 end of *each* frankfurter. Set aside.

1 cup cornmeal
⅔ cup all-purpose flour
2 tablespoons sugar
1½ teaspoons baking powder
¼ teaspoon onion powder
1 beaten egg
¾ cup milk
1 tablespoon cooking oil

● For batter, in a mixing bowl combine cornmeal, flour, sugar, baking powder, and onion powder. Stir together egg, milk, and oil. Add liquid ingredients to dry ingredients; mix well. (Batter will be thick.) Transfer batter to a pie plate.

Cooking oil *or* shortening for deep-fat frying
Mustard, catsup, *or* barbecue sauce (optional)

● In a large skillet heat ¾ inch of oil or melted shortening to 365°. Dip frankfurters in batter, turning to coat. Fry frankfurters, a few at a time, in hot oil. Turn after 10 seconds to prevent batter from sliding off. Cook 2 to 3 minutes more, turning again after 1 minute.

Drain frankfurters on paper towels. Keep warm in a 300° oven while frying remaining frankfurters. If desired, serve with mustard, catsup, or barbecue sauce. Serves 4 or 5.

Nutrition information per serving: 1,026 calories, 21 g protein, 55 g carbohydrate, 80 g fat (19 g saturated), 115 mg cholesterol, 1,420 mg sodium, 357 mg potassium.

Curried Corn Dogs
3 to 4 teaspoons curry powder
Chutney (optional)

Prepare Corn Dogs as above, *except* stir curry powder in with the cornmeal. Serve with chutney, if desired.

Beans and Brats with Biscuits

Mustard Biscuits
½ **cup chopped onion**
¼ **cup water**
1 **clove garlic, minced**

● Prepare and bake Mustard Biscuits. Set aside.

Meanwhile, in a saucepan combine onion, water, and garlic. Bring to boiling; reduce heat. Cover; simmer 5 minutes or till tender. *Do not drain.*

---

1 **15-ounce can navy beans *or* great northern beans**
1 **8½-ounce can lima beans *or* one 8-ounce can red kidney beans, drained**
½ **cup catsup**
¼ **cup honey *or* maple-flavored syrup**
1 **tablespoon cider vinegar**
⅛ **teaspoon pepper**
12 **ounces fully cooked smoked bratwurst, cut into ½-inch slices, *or* one 12-ounce package fully cooked smoked sausage links, cut into ½-inch slices**

● Stir in *undrained* navy or great northern beans, drained lima or red kidney beans, catsup, honey or syrup, vinegar, and pepper. Stir in bratwurst or sausage links. Bring to boiling; reduce heat. Cover and simmer for 5 minutes. Uncover and simmer for 5 minutes more or to desired consistency.

---

1 **large apple, chopped (1 cup)**

● Stir in apple. Cover and cook 2 minutes more or till apple is just tender. Serve with Mustard Biscuits. Makes 4 servings.

Nutrition information per serving: 772 calories, 24 g protein, 82 g carbohydrate, 40 g fat (13 g saturated), 62 mg cholesterol, 1,557 mg sodium, 831 mg potassium.

Mustard Biscuits
¾ **cup all-purpose flour**
1 **teaspoon baking powder**
½ **teaspoon sugar**
¼ **teaspoon cream of tartar**
¼ **cup shortening, margarine, *or* butter**
⅓ **cup milk**
1 **tablespoon prepared mustard**

Combine flour, baking powder, sugar, and cream of tartar. Cut in shortening, margarine, or butter till mixture resembles coarse crumbs. Make a well in the center. Stir together milk and mustard; add to dry ingredients all at once. Stir just till dough clings together. Drop dough from a tablespoon into 8 mounds on a greased baking sheet. Bake in a 400° oven for 10 to 12 minutes or till golden.

Make It Easy
1 **cup packaged biscuit mix**

Prepare Beans and Brats with Biscuits as above, *except* for Mustard Biscuits omit the flour, baking powder, sugar, cream of tartar, and shortening, margarine, or butter. In a small mixing bowl stir together the packaged biscuit mix, milk, and mustard. Continue as above.

Nutrition information per serving: 690 calories, 24 g protein, 82 g carbohydrate, 31 g fat (10 g saturated), 62 mg cholesterol, 1,821 mg sodium, 822 mg potassium.

Pork Tenderloin Sandwiches

¾ **pound pork tenderloin**
¼ **cup all-purpose flour**
¼ **teaspoon onion *or* garlic powder**
¼ **teaspoon pepper**
1 **beaten egg**
1 **tablespoon milk *or* water**
1 **cup finely crushed rich round crackers (about 24) *or* ¾ cup fine dry bread crumbs**

● Cut pork crosswise into 4 slices. With a meat mallet, pound each pork slice between plastic wrap to ¼-inch thickness.

In a shallow bowl combine flour, onion powder, and pepper. In another shallow bowl combine egg and milk or water. In a third bowl place crushed crackers. Dip *each* pork slice into the flour mixture, coating well, then into the egg mixture, and then into the crumbs to coat.

1 **tablespoon cooking oil**
4 **hamburger buns, large buns, *or* kaiser rolls, split and toasted**
Mustard, catsup, onion slices, dill pickle slices, *and/or* roasted red peppers (optional)

● In a large skillet cook 2 pork slices in hot oil over medium heat for 6 to 8 minutes or till pork is no longer pink, turning once. Remove from skillet; keep warm. Repeat with remaining slices, adding more oil, if necessary.

Place on buns. If desired, serve with mustard, catsup, onion, pickle, and/or peppers. Serves 4.

Nutrition information per serving: 405 calories, 26 g protein, 40 g carbohydrate, 15 g fat (4 g saturated), 114 mg cholesterol, 477 mg sodium, 460 mg potassium.

Italian-Style Pork Tenderloin
1 **teaspoon dried Italian seasoning, crushed**
4 **slices mozzarella cheese**
¼ **cup pizza sauce**

Prepare Pork Tenderloin Sandwiches as above, *except* add Italian seasoning to flour mixture. Place breaded, cooked pork slices on the unheated rack of a broiler pan. Place *one* slice of cheese on *each*. Broil 3 to 4 inches from the heat for 30 to 60 seconds or till cheese is melted. Top with pizza sauce. If desired, place on buns.

Nutrition information per serving: 357 calories, 30 g protein, 20 g carbohydrate, 18 g fat (6 g saturated), 130 mg cholesterol, 401 mg sodium, 429 mg potassium.

Use the flat side of a meat mallet to pound the pork to ¼-inch thickness. Tender pieces of meat such as pork or beef tenderloin or chicken breasts don't need to be tenderized, just flattened. So the flat side of the mallet should be used instead of the coarse side.

Ham and Bean Soup

1 cup dry navy beans *or* black-eyed
  peas
4 cups water

● Rinse beans. In a Dutch oven combine beans and water. Bring to boiling; reduce heat. Simmer, uncovered, for 2 minutes. Remove from heat. Cover and let stand for 1 hour. (*Or,* skip boiling water and soak beans overnight in a covered pan.) Drain and rinse beans.

1¼ to 1½ pounds meaty smoked pork
  hocks
4 cups water
2 cups chopped onion
1 tablespoon instant chicken bouillon
  granules
1 tablespoon snipped fresh parsley
1 tablespoon snipped fresh basil *or*
  oregano *or* 1 teaspoon dried basil
  or oregano, crushed
1 tablespoon snipped fresh thyme *or*
  1 teaspoon dried thyme, crushed
2 cloves garlic, minced
2 bay leaves

● Meanwhile, trim separable fat from meat. In the Dutch oven combine beans, meat, 4 cups *fresh water,* onion, bouillon granules, parsley, basil or oregano, thyme, garlic, and bay leaves. Bring to boiling; reduce heat. Cover and simmer for 1¾ hours. Remove pork hocks; set aside to cool. Mash beans slightly.

1½ cups sliced celery
1 cup sliced carrots

● Add celery and carrots to the bean mixture in the Dutch oven. Return to boiling; reduce heat. Cover and simmer for 15 minutes.
  Meanwhile, cut meat off bones and coarsely chop. Discard bones. Remove bay leaves; discard. Stir the meat into the bean mixture in the Dutch oven. Heat through. Serves 4.

Nutrition information per serving: 290 calories, 17 g protein, 46 g carbohydrate, 5 g fat (2 g saturated), 13 mg cholesterol, 997 mg sodium, 876 mg potassium.

Make It Easy
3 cups water
2 15-ounce cans navy beans
2 cups loose-pack frozen broccoli,
  cauliflower, and carrots
2 cups cubed fully cooked ham
  (10 ounces)

Prepare Ham and Bean Soup as above, *except* omit dry beans, pork hocks, celery, and carrots. Reduce water to 3 cups. In a Dutch oven combine water, *undrained* canned beans, onion, bouillon granules, parsley, basil or oregano, thyme, garlic, and bay leaves. Cover and simmer for 15 minutes.
  Mash beans slightly. Stir in the frozen vegetables and the ham. Bring to boiling; reduce heat. Cover and simmer for 5 minutes or till vegetables are crisp tender. Remove bay leaves; discard.

Nutrition information per serving: 334 calories, 30 g protein, 43 g carbohydrate, 5 g fat (2 g saturated), 39 mg cholesterol, 1,912 mg sodium, 911 mg potassium.

Peppered Pot Roast

For Fruit-Sauced Pot Roast, fix Peppered Pot Roast as directed, except add water to the pan juices to equal 1½ cups. Stir ½ cup mixed dried fruit bits and 2 tablespoons brown sugar into the pan juices with the flour mixture.

1 1½- to 2-pound beef chuck pot roast
1 teaspoon lemon pepper *or* ½ teaspoon cracked pepper
1 tablespoon cooking oil

● Trim separable fat from roast. Rub 1 side with lemon pepper or pepper. In a Dutch oven brown roast on all sides in hot oil. Drain off fat.

½ cup water
¼ cup tomato juice
¼ cup dry white wine, beer, *or* water
1 teaspoon instant beef bouillon granules
½ teaspoon dried thyme, crushed

● Combine ½ cup water; tomato juice; ¼ cup wine, beer, or water; bouillon granules; and thyme. Pour around roast in Dutch oven. Bring to boiling; reduce heat. Cover and simmer 1 hour. Or, bake, covered, in a 325° oven 1 hour.

4 medium carrots, cut into 1½-inch pieces
2 medium potatoes, peeled and quartered
1 medium onion, cut into wedges

● Add carrots, potatoes, and onion to meat. Cover and simmer or bake 45 to 60 minutes more or till tender, adding additional water, if necessary. Transfer meat and vegetables to a serving platter. Cover to keep warm.

⅓ cup cold water
3 tablespoons all-purpose flour

● For gravy, pour pan juices into a large measuring cup. Skim off fat; discard. If necessary, add water to pan juices to equal 1¼ cups. Return to the Dutch oven. Stir together cold water and flour. Stir into juices in Dutch oven. Cook and stir till thickened and bubbly. Cook and stir 1 minute more. Season to taste with salt and pepper. Serve with meat and vegetables. Makes 4 to 6 servings.

Nutrition information per serving: 432 calories, 34 g protein, 28 g carbohydrate, 19 g fat (7 g saturated), 105 mg cholesterol, 587 mg sodium, 796 mg potassium.

Gingersnap Pot Roast

2 medium sweet potatoes, peeled and quartered
1 10-ounce package frozen brussels sprouts, rinsed to separate, *or* 2 cups fresh brussels sprouts
¼ cup crushed gingersnaps (4 or 5)
1 tablespoon brown sugar

Prepare Peppered Pot Roast as above, *except* omit the potatoes and carrots. Add sweet potatoes with the onion. Cover and simmer or bake for 30 minutes. Add the brussels sprouts. Cover and simmer or bake for 15 to 30 minutes more or till tender. Omit the flour-water mixture. Stir the gingersnaps and brown sugar into the pan juices. Continue as above.

Nutrition information per serving: 495 calories, 36 g protein, 41 g carbohydrate, 20 g fat (7 g saturated), 105 mg cholesterol, 627 mg sodium, 755 mg potassium.

Home-Style Beef and Noodles

Many Beef-and-Noodles fans wouldn't dream of indulging in this saucy dish without spooning it over a generous scoop of mashed potatoes.

1 pound boneless beef round steak, trimmed of separable fat and cut into ¾-inch cubes
1 tablespoon cooking oil
½ cup chopped onion
2 cloves garlic
4 cups beef broth
2 tablespoons vinegar
½ teaspoon dried marjoram *or* basil, crushed
¼ teaspoon pepper

● In a large saucepan brown *half* of the meat in hot oil. Remove from saucepan. Brown the remaining meat with the onion and garlic, adding more oil, if necessary. Drain off *excess* fat.

Return all meat and vegetables to the saucepan. Stir in 4 cups beef broth, vinegar, marjoram or basil, and pepper. Bring to boiling; reduce heat. Cover and simmer for 1 to 1¼ hours or till meat is tender.

8 ounces frozen noodles

● Stir noodles into beef and broth mixture. Bring to boiling; reduce heat. Cook, uncovered, 25 to 30 minutes or till noodles are tender. Drain meat and noodles from broth, reserving *2½ cups* of the broth. (If necessary, add additional broth or water to make 2½ cups.)

¼ cup beef broth
3 tablespoons all-purpose flour
2 tablespoons snipped fresh parsley (optional)

● Return the reserved broth mixture to the saucepan. Combine the ¼ cup beef broth and the flour. Stir mixture into reserved liquid in the saucepan. Cook and stir till thickened and bubbly. Cook and stir for 1 minute more. Stir in beef and noodles; heat through. If desired, garnish with parsley. Makes 4 servings.

Nutrition information per serving: 402 calories, 33 g protein, 38 g carbohydrate, 13 g fat (3 g saturated), 100 mg cholesterol, 897 mg sodium, 590 mg potassium.

Savory Almond Meatballs

Share this impressive pasta sauce and meat combination with friends and family.

1 egg white
2 tablespoons milk
¼ teaspoon pepper
⅛ teaspoon dried thyme, crushed
½ cup finely chopped onion
⅓ cup finely crushed zwieback *or* fine dry bread crumbs
¼ cup chopped toasted almonds
¼ cup snipped fresh parsley
1 pound ground beef *or* ground pork
2 tablespoons margarine *or* butter

● To make meatballs, in a mixing bowl combine egg white, the 2 tablespoons milk, ¼ teaspoon pepper, and thyme. Stir in onion, zwieback or bread crumbs, almonds, and the ¼ cup parsley. Add the meat; mix well. Shape into 30 meatballs.

In a large skillet cook meatballs, half at a time, in margarine or butter over medium heat about 10 minutes or till no pink remains, turning often. Remove meatballs from skillet, reserving *2 tablespoons* of the drippings in the skillet. Drain the meatballs on paper towels.

2 tablespoons all-purpose flour
2 teaspoons instant beef bouillon granules
⅛ teaspoon pepper
2 cups milk
2½ cups hot cooked spinach noodles *or* hot cooked noodles
Snipped fresh parsley (optional)

● For sauce, stir flour, bouillon granules, and ⅛ teaspoon pepper into the reserved drippings. Add the 2 cups milk all at once. Cook and stir till thickened and bubbly. Cook and stir 1 minute more. Return the meatballs to skillet. Heat through. Serve over hot cooked noodles. If desired, garnish with parsley. Serves 5.

Nutrition information per serving: 460 calories, 30 g protein, 36 g carbohydrate, 21 g fat (7 g saturated), 101 mg cholesterol, 546 mg sodium, 482 mg potassium.

Oven Directions: Prepare Savory Almond Meatballs as above, *except* place meatballs in an 11x7x2-inch baking dish. Bake in a 375° oven for 20 to 25 minutes or till no pink remains. Drain meatballs on paper towels.

For sauce, in a medium saucepan melt the margarine or butter. Stir in flour, bouillon granules, and ⅛ teaspoon pepper. Add the 2 cups milk all at once. Cook and stir till thickened and bubbly. Cook and stir 1 minute more. Add the baked meatballs and heat through. Serve as above.

Try this method of shaping meatballs to get the right number of meatballs in a uniform size. Pat the meat mixture into a 6x5-inch rectangle on a piece of waxed paper. Divide the rectangle into 30 squares. Roll each square into a meatball.

Meat Loaf

Update yesterday's meat loaf by giving it today's great grilled flavor.

1 beaten egg
¼ cup fine dry bread crumbs, quick-cooking oats, *or* toasted wheat germ
¼ cup finely chopped onion
¼ cup vegetable juice cocktail, tomato juice, *or* milk
1 tablespoon prepared mustard, horseradish mustard, *or* Dijon-style mustard
¼ teaspoon salt
¼ teaspoon pepper
1 pound lean ground beef *or* ground pork

● In a mixing bowl stir together egg; bread crumbs, oats, or wheat germ; onion; vegetable juice cocktail, tomato juice, or milk; mustard; salt; and pepper. Add ground beef or pork; mix well.

In a shallow baking pan or dish pat the meat mixture into a 7x3x2-inch loaf. Bake in a 350° oven for 45 to 50 minutes or till no pink remains.

---

2 tablespoons catsup
1 tablespoon honey
½ teaspoon lemon juice

● Meanwhile, in a mixing bowl stir together catsup, honey, and lemon juice. Spread over top of meat loaf just before serving. Serves 4.

Nutrition information per serving: 290 calories, 27 g protein, 13 g carbohydrate, 14 g fat (5 g saturated), 137 mg cholesterol, 440 mg sodium, 343 mg potassium.

Ham Loaf
½ pound ground fully cooked ham
¾ cup soft bread crumbs

Prepare Meat Loaf as above, *except* substitute ham for ½ pound of the ground beef or pork and use soft bread crumbs instead of the dry bread crumbs, oats, or toasted wheat germ.

Nutrition information per serving: 271 calories, 29 g protein, 13 g carbohydrate, 11 g fat (4 g saturated), 126 mg cholesterol, 1,165 mg sodium, 409 mg potassium.

Grill Directions: Prepare Meat Loaf as above, *except* on a piece of waxed paper shape the meat mixture into a 5- to 6-inch round loaf.

In a covered grill arrange preheated coals around a drip pan. Test for *medium* heat above the pan. (See tip, page 35.) Carefully invert loaf onto the grill rack over the drip pan, but not over the coals. Peel off waxed paper. Lower the grill hood. Grill for 30 to 40 minutes or till no pink remains. Continue as above.

Double-Crust Pizza Casserole

Simplify your schedule by making this hearty casserole up to 24 hours ahead. Cover and chill the prepared casserole; then bake it as directed in the recipe.

1½ **cups all-purpose flour**
1½ **cups packaged instant mashed**
  potatoes
 1 **cup milk**
¼ **cup margarine *or* butter, melted**

● For pizza crust, in a mixing bowl combine the flour, instant mashed potatoes, milk, and margarine or butter. Set mixture aside.

½ **pound ground beef**
½ **pound bulk Italian *or* pork sausage**
½ **cup chopped onion**
 1 **8-ounce can tomato sauce**
½ **cup sliced pitted ripe olives**
  (optional)
½ **teaspoon dried basil, crushed**
½ **teaspoon dried oregano, crushed**
⅛ **teaspoon garlic powder**
⅛ **teaspoon pepper**

● For filling, in a large skillet cook beef, sausage, and onion till meats are no longer pink. Drain off fat. Stir in tomato sauce, olives (if desired), basil, oregano, garlic powder, and pepper.

 1 **cup shredded mozzarella cheese**
  (4 ounces)

● Press *half* of the crust onto the bottom and up the sides of a greased 8x8x2-inch baking dish. Spread filling over crust; sprinkle with cheese. Roll remaining crust between 2 sheets of floured waxed paper into a 10x10-inch square. Remove top sheet of waxed paper. Invert crust over filling in dish. Peel off second sheet of waxed paper. Trim edges as necessary. Turn edges under and press onto bottom crust to seal. Cut slits in top crust for steam to escape.

● Bake in a 425° oven for 30 to 35 minutes or till heated through and crust is golden. Let stand 10 minutes before serving. Serves 6.

Nutrition information per serving: 461 calories, 23 g protein, 40 g carbohydrate, 24 g fat (8 g saturated), 57 mg cholesterol, 699 mg sodium, 563 mg potassium.

Make It Easy
 1 **cup pizza *or* spaghetti sauce**

Prepare Double-Crust Pizza Casserole as above, *except* substitute pizza or spaghetti sauce for the tomato sauce, basil, oregano, garlic powder, and pepper.

Nutrition information per serving: 471 calories, 23 g protein, 40 g carbohydrate, 24 g fat (8 g saturated), 57 mg cholesterol, 639 mg sodium, 417 mg potassium.

BIRTHDAY DINNERS

*S*urprise a friend with a dressed-up dinner on his or her special day. Add a festive touch to your table with some splashy decorations.

MENU

●

BEEF STROGANOFF WITH SQUASH
(page 23)

CONFETTI ANGEL FOOD CAKE
(page 94)

Beef Stroganoff

Named after a nineteenth-century Russian diplomat, Count P. Stroganoff, this sour cream sauce enhanced with beef, mushrooms, and onions has enchanted Americans for years.

1 **pound beef round steak**
1 **tablespoon cooking oil**
1 **medium green or sweet red pepper, cut into bite-size strips**
1 **medium onion, sliced and separated into rings**
1 **clove garlic, minced**
2 **cups sliced fresh mushrooms**
½ **cup beef broth**
½ **cup tomato juice**
2 **tablespoons dry red wine**
¼ **teaspoon pepper**

● Trim separable fat from meat. Partially freeze meat. Thinly slice across the grain into bite-size strips. In a large skillet brown *half* of the meat in hot oil with green pepper. Remove meat and pepper from skillet. Brown remaining meat with onion and garlic, adding more oil, if necessary. Drain off fat. Return all meat, green pepper, onion, and garlic to skillet.

Stir in mushrooms, beef broth, tomato juice, red wine, and pepper. Bring to boiling; reduce heat. Cover and simmer for 30 to 45 minutes or till meat is tender.

2 **cups medium noodles**
2 **cups loose-pack frozen cauliflower, broccoli, and carrots**
1 **8-ounce carton dairy sour cream or plain yogurt**
2 **tablespoons all-purpose flour**

● Meanwhile, cook noodles and vegetables in a large amount of boiling water for 6 to 8 minutes or till tender. Drain; keep warm.

Combine sour cream and flour. Stir into meat mixture. Cook and stir over medium heat till bubbly. Cook and stir 1 minute more. Serve over noodles and vegetables. Makes 4 servings.

Nutrition information per serving: 443 calories, 30 g protein, 31 g carbohydrate, 22 g fat (10 g saturated), 116 mg cholesterol, 328 mg sodium, 871 mg potassium.

Beef Stroganoff with Squash
1 **medium spaghetti squash (2½ to 3 pounds)**

Prepare Beef Stroganoff as above, *except* omit noodles and frozen vegetables. Halve spaghetti squash lengthwise; scoop out seeds. Place squash, cut side down, in a baking dish. Bake in a 350° oven for 30 to 40 minutes or till tender. Using a fork, scrape the squash from the shells to form spaghettilike strands. Serve stroganoff over the squash.

Nutrition information per serving: 426 calories, 27 g protein, 30 g carbohydrate, 22 g fat (10 g saturated), 86 mg cholesterol, 341 mg sodium, 997 mg potassium.

Autumn Beef Stew

Welcome the chilly days of fall with a simmering pot of stew filled with meat, vegetables, and fruit.

1 **pound beef** *or* **pork stew meat, cut into ¾-inch cubes**
3 **tablespoons cooking oil**
3½ **cups water**
1 **medium onion, cut into thin wedges**
¾ **cup apple juice** *or* **apple cider**
2 **tablespoons instant beef bouillon granules**
1 **tablespoon vinegar**
1½ **teaspoons snipped fresh basil** *or* **½ teaspoon dried basil, crushed**
1 **teaspoon snipped fresh thyme** *or* **¼ teaspoon dried thyme, crushed**
¼ **teaspoon pepper**

● In a Dutch oven brown meat, half at a time, in hot oil. Drain off fat. Stir in water, onion, the ¾ cup apple juice or cider, bouillon granules, vinegar, basil, and pepper. Bring to boiling; reduce heat. Cover and simmer for 1 hour.

2 **medium carrots, cut into 1-inch pieces**
2 **cups peeled, cubed butternut squash**
1 **large pear** *or* **apple, cored and coarsely chopped (1 cup)**
½ **cup apple juice** *or* **apple cider**
⅓ **cup all-purpose flour**

● Stir in carrots. Simmer, covered, for 15 minutes. Add squash and pear or apple. Simmer, covered, about 10 minutes more or till meat and vegetables are tender.

Combine the ½ cup apple juice or apple cider and flour. Stir into meat mixture. Cook and stir till thickened and bubbly. Cook and stir 1 minute more. Makes 5 servings.

Nutrition information per serving: 468 calories, 26 g protein, 39 g carbohydrate, 23 g fat (6 g saturated), 79 mg cholesterol, 1,465 mg sodium, 968 mg potassium.

Crockery Cooker Directions: Prepare and brown meat as above. In the bottom of a 3½- to 4-quart crockery cooker, layer meat, onion, squash, and carrots. Decrease the water to 3 cups. Stir together the water, ¾ cup apple juice or cider, bouillon granules, vinegar, basil, thyme, and pepper. Pour over meat and vegetables in crockery cooker. Cover and cook on low-heat setting for 9 to 11 hours or on high-heat setting for 4½ to 5½ hours. Combine the ½ cup apple juice or cider and the flour; stir into the meat mixture along with the pear or apple. Cover and cook on high-heat setting for 30 minutes or till bubbly.

Vegetable Beef Soup

Sip a spoonful of this herbed tomato broth filled to the rim with meat and vegetables. It's "souper" delicious.

¾ **pound beef *or* pork stew meat, cut into ½-inch cubes**
1 **tablespoon cooking oil**
3 **cups water**
1 **16-ounce can tomatoes, cut up**
1 **tablespoon instant beef bouillon granules**
2 **teaspoons Worcestershire sauce**
½ **teaspoon dried marjoram, crushed**
½ **teaspoon dried oregano, crushed**
¼ **teaspoon pepper**
1 **bay leaf**

● In a large saucepan or Dutch oven brown meat in hot oil. Drain off fat. Stir in water, *undrained* tomatoes, bouillon granules, Worcestershire sauce, marjoram, oregano, pepper, and bay leaf. Bring to boiling; reduce heat. Cover and simmer 20 minutes.

1 **medium potato, peeled and cubed (½ cup) *or* ½ cup loose-pack frozen hash brown potatoes**
½ **of a 9-ounce package frozen baby lima beans**
1 **cup loose-pack frozen whole kernel corn**
½ **cup sliced carrot**
⅓ **cup chopped onion**

● Stir in potato, lima beans, corn, carrot, and onion. Return to boiling; reduce heat. Cover and simmer for 25 to 30 minutes more or till the vegetables and the meat are tender. Discard bay leaf. Makes 4 servings.

Nutrition information per serving: 323 calories, 23 g protein, 30 g carbohydrate, 13 g fat (4 g saturated), 60 mg cholesterol, 976 mg sodium, 768 mg potassium.

Make It Easy
¾ **pound lean ground beef**

Prepare Vegetable Beef Soup as above, *except* omit the stew meat and oil. Cook the ground beef in a large saucepan or Dutch oven till no longer pink. Drain off fat. Stir in remaining ingredients and simmer for 25 to 30 minutes or till vegetables are tender. Discard bay leaf.

Cutting up canned tomatoes is a simple task if you use a pair of kitchen shears. Snip the tomatoes right in the can; then add them to the recipe.

Beefy Chili with Beans

Experiment to find your tolerance for chili explosives. Try the green chili peppers if you suspect a low tolerance and jalapeños if you like it hot.

1½ **pounds boneless beef top round steak**
 1 **tablespoon cooking oil**
 1 **cup chopped onion**
 2 **cloves garlic, minced**

● Partially freeze meat. Thinly slice across the grain into bite-size strips. In a Dutch oven brown *half* of the meat in hot oil. Remove from pan. Brown remaining meat with the onion and garlic, adding more oil, if necessary. Drain off fat. Return all meat, onion, and garlic to pan.

 2 **16-ounce cans tomatoes, cut up**
 1 **cup beef broth**
 1 **4-ounce can diced green chili peppers** *or* ⅓ **cup chopped, canned jalapeño chili peppers**
 2 **tablespoons chili powder**
 1 **tablespoon brown sugar**
 2 **teaspoons dried oregano, crushed**
 1 **teaspoon salt**
 1 **teaspoon ground cumin**

● Stir in the *undrained* tomatoes, beef broth, green chili peppers or jalapeño peppers, chili powder, brown sugar, oregano, salt, and cumin. Bring mixture to boiling; reduce heat. Cover and simmer for 1 hour or till meat is tender.

 2 **15-ounce cans pinto beans** *or* **red kidney beans, drained**
   Dairy sour cream *or* **shredded cheddar cheese (optional)**

● Stir in the beans and cook for 5 minutes more. If desired, top with sour cream or cheddar cheese. Makes 6 servings.

Nutrition information per serving: 362 calories, 32 g protein, 39 g carbohydrate, 9 g fat (3 g saturated), 62 mg cholesterol, 1,093 mg sodium, 1,239 mg potassium.

Make It Easy
1½ **pounds ground beef**

Prepare Beefy Chili with Beans as above, *except* substitute the ground beef for the top round steak. Omit the cooking oil. In a Dutch oven cook the ground beef with the onion and garlic till meat is no longer pink. Drain off fat. Stir in beans and the remaining ingredients, *except* for the sour cream or cheese.

Bring mixture to boiling; reduce heat. Cover and simmer for 15 minutes. Uncover and simmer for 10 minutes more or to desired consistency. Serve as above.

Nutrition information per serving: 424 calories, 34 g protein, 39 g carbohydrate, 16 g fat (5 g saturated), 81 mg cholesterol, 1,092 mg sodium, 1,167 mg potassium.

Hamburgers

The hamburger on a bun has been regarded as a classic American sandwich since it was sold by an enterprising merchant at the St. Louis Exposition of 1904.

1 pound ground beef, ground pork, *or* ground turkey
2 tablespoons catsup
1 teaspoon prepared mustard
1 teaspoon Worcestershire sauce
½ teaspoon onion salt *or* garlic salt
¼ teaspoon pepper

● In a mixing bowl mix together the ground beef, pork, or turkey; catsup; mustard; Worcestershire sauce; onion salt; and pepper.

Shape meat mixture into four ½- or ¾-inch-thick patties. Place patties on the unheated rack of a broiler pan. Broil 3 to 4 inches from the heat till no pink remains, turning once. Allow 10 to 12 minutes for ½-inch-thick patties or 15 to 18 minutes for ¾-inch-thick patties.

4 slices American, Swiss, cheddar, *or* brick cheese (optional)
4 hamburger buns, split and toasted
Catsup, mustard, *and/or* pickle slices (optional)

● If desired, top burgers with a slice of cheese. Broil just till cheese melts. Place burgers on toasted buns. If desired, serve with catsup, mustard, and/or pickle slices. Makes 4 servings.

Nutrition information per serving: 351 calories, 23 g protein, 25 g carbohydrate, 17 g fat (6 g saturated), 68 mg cholesterol, 652 mg sodium, 338 mg potassium.

Teriyaki Burgers
½ cup finely chopped water chestnuts
2 tablespoons teriyaki sauce
1 tablespoon sesame seeds, toasted
¼ cup plum preserves

Prepare Hamburgers as above, *except* omit catsup, mustard, and Worcestershire sauce. Do not use the cheese.

Mix the water chestnuts, teriyaki sauce, and *2 teaspoons* of the sesame seeds into the meat mixture. Broil or grill as directed.

Meanwhile, for sauce, in a small saucepan heat preserves with the remaining sesame seeds over low heat till preserves are melted. Serve sauce over burgers. If desired, serve on buns.

Nutrition information per serving: 424 calories, 24 g protein, 41 g carbohydrate, 18 g fat (6 g saturated), 68 mg cholesterol, 880 mg sodium, 368 mg potassium.

Grill Directions: Prepare Hamburgers as above, *except* grill patties on an uncovered grill directly over *medium-hot* coals till no pink remains, turning once. (See tip, page 35.) Allow 10 to 12 minutes for ½-inch-thick patties or 15 to 18 minutes for ¾-inch-thick patties. If desired, top burgers with cheese. Serve as above.

Sloppy Joes

¾ **pound ground beef, ground pork, *or* ground turkey**
½ **cup chopped onion**
½ **cup chopped celery**
1 **clove garlic, minced**
1 **8-ounce can tomato sauce**
¼ **cup chili sauce *or* catsup**
1 **tablespoon brown sugar**
2 **teaspoons prepared mustard**
1 **teaspoon Worcestershire sauce**

● In a large skillet cook ground beef, pork, or turkey; onion; celery; and garlic till meat is no longer pink and onion is tender. Drain off fat. Stir in tomato sauce, chili sauce or catsup, brown sugar, mustard, and Worcestershire sauce. Bring to boiling; reduce heat. Cover and simmer for 10 minutes.

4 **hamburger buns, split and toasted**
2 **tablespoons shredded cheddar cheese**

● To serve, spoon meat mixture over buns and sprinkle with cheese. Makes 4 servings.

Nutrition information per serving: 359 calories, 20 g protein, 37 g carbohydrate, 15 g fat (5 g saturated), 53 mg cholesterol, 969 mg sodium, 603 mg potassium.

Microwave Directions: In a 1½-quart microwave-safe casserole combine ground meat, onion, celery, and garlic. Micro-cook, covered, on 100% power (high) for 5 to 7 minutes or till meat is no longer pink and vegetables are tender, stirring once. Drain off fat. Stir in tomato sauce, chili sauce or catsup, brown sugar, mustard, and Worcestershire sauce. Cook, covered, on high for 3 to 5 minutes more or till heated through. Serve as above.

Pizza Crust

2¾ **to 3¼ cups all-purpose flour**
1 **package active dry yeast**
½ **teaspoon salt**
1 **cup warm water (120° to 130°)**
2 **tablespoons cooking oil**

● For crust, in a large mixing bowl combine *1¼ cups* of the flour, the yeast, and salt. Add warm water and oil. Beat with an electric mixer on low speed for 30 seconds, scraping sides of the bowl constantly. Beat on high speed for 3 minutes. Using a spoon, stir in as much of the remaining flour as you can. Turn out onto a lightly floured surface. Knead in enough of the remaining flour to make a moderately stiff dough that is smooth and elastic (6 to 8 minutes total). Divide dough in half. Cover; let rest 10 minutes.

Pizza

Cornmeal (optional)
Pizza Crust (see recipe, page 28)

● Grease two 12-inch pizza pans or baking sheets. If desired, sprinkle each with cornmeal. On a lightly floured surface, roll *each half* of Pizza Crust dough into a 13-inch circle. Transfer to pizza pans. Build up edges slightly. *Do not* let rise. Bake in a 425° oven for 10 to 12 minutes or till lightly browned.

Meat Topping *or* Cheese Topping

● Top crusts with Meat Topping or Cheese Topping. Bake pizzas in a 425° oven for 10 to 15 minutes or till bubbly. Serves 6 to 8.

Meat Topping

1 15-ounce can or one 15½-ounce jar pizza sauce
1 pound ground beef, *or* bulk Italian *or* pork sausage, cooked and drained
2 medium tomatoes, thinly sliced
1 medium onion, thinly sliced
2 small green peppers, thinly sliced
2 cups shredded mozzarella cheese (8 ounces)
1 cup sliced fresh mushrooms
½ cup sliced pitted ripe olives
¼ cup grated Parmesan *or* Romano cheese

Spread pizza sauce over hot crusts. Sprinkle with ground beef or sausage. Arrange tomato slices, onion slices, and green pepper slices atop. Sprinkle with mozzarella cheese, mushrooms, olives, and Parmesan or Romano cheese.

Nutrition information per serving: 594 calories, 30 g protein, 56 g carbohydrate, 28 g fat (10 g saturated), 62 mg cholesterol, 1,176 mg sodium, 457 mg potassium.

Cheese Topping

2 cups shredded mozzarella cheese (8 ounces)
1½ cups ricotta cheese
½ cup grated Parmesan or Romano cheese
3 tablespoons milk
½ teaspoon dried Italian seasoning, crushed
4 medium red or yellow tomatoes, thinly sliced
2 small green peppers, thinly sliced

Stir together the mozzarella cheese, ricotta cheese, Parmesan or Romano cheese, milk, and Italian seasoning. Spread over hot crusts. Arrange tomato and green pepper slices over the cheese mixture.

Nutrition information per serving: 512 calories, 27 g protein, 53 g carbohydrate, 22 g fat (11 g saturated), 58 mg cholesterol, 455 mg sodium, 419 mg potassium.

Lasagna

Freeze leftover single-servings of Lasagna in lightly greased individual casseroles. Bake one frozen casserole, covered, in a 375° oven for 50 minutes. Uncover and bake 10 minutes more or till hot.

1 pound ground beef, ground pork, bulk pork sausage, *or* bulk Italian sausage
½ cup chopped onion
½ cup sliced fresh mushrooms
2 cloves garlic, minced
1 16-ounce can whole Italian-style tomatoes, cut up, *or* one 16-ounce can tomatoes, cut up
1 6-ounce can tomato paste
1 teaspoon dried basil, crushed
1 teaspoon dried oregano, crushed
½ teaspoon fennel seed, crushed (optional)
¼ teaspoon pepper

● For sauce, in a large saucepan cook meat, onion, mushrooms, and garlic till meat is browned and onion is tender. Drain off fat. Stir in *undrained* tomatoes, tomato paste, basil, oregano, fennel seed (if desired), and pepper.

Bring to boiling; reduce heat. Cover and simmer for 15 minutes, stirring occasionally.

8 lasagna noodles

● Meanwhile, cook lasagna noodles according to package directions. Drain.

1 beaten egg
1 15-ounce container ricotta cheese
½ cup grated Parmesan cheese
⅓ cup whipping cream, light cream, *or* milk
1 tablespoon dried parsley flakes
¼ teaspoon pepper
1½ cups shredded mozzarella cheese (6 ounces)
⅓ cup whipping cream, light cream, *or* milk

● For filling, in a bowl combine egg, ricotta cheese, Parmesan cheese, ⅓ cup cream, parsley, and pepper.

Arrange *half* of the cooked noodles in a 12x7½x2-inch baking dish. Spread with *one-third* of the filling. Top with *half* of the sauce, and *half* of the mozzarella cheese. Continue layering with remaining noodles, *one-third* of the filling, and remaining sauce. To the last portion of filling, stir in ⅓ cup cream or milk. Pour over layers. (If desired, cover and chill lasagna for up to 24 hours.)

Bake, uncovered, in a 375° oven for 30 to 35 minutes or till heated through. Sprinkle with remaining mozzarella cheese. Let stand 15 minutes before serving. Makes 10 servings.

Nutrition information per serving: 378 calories, 25 g protein, 22 g carbohydrate, 21 g fat (12 g saturated), 110 mg cholesterol, 308 mg sodium, 503 mg potassium.

Cottage Cheese Lasagna
1 12-ounce container cream-style cottage cheese

Prepare Lasagna as above, *except* substitute the *undrained* cottage cheese for the ricotta cheese and the first ⅓ cup whipping cream.

Nutrition information per serving: 312 calories, 24 g protein, 21 g carbohydrate, 14 g fat (7 g saturated), 83 mg cholesterol, 407 mg sodium, 481 mg potassium.

Spaghetti and Meatballs

Thomas Jefferson introduced spaghetti to America when he returned from Italy with a die for making pasta. But not until the early 1900s when the wheat needed for pasta production was grown here, was spaghetti commercially produced in this country.

1 **cup sliced fresh mushrooms**
 ½ **cup chopped onion**
 ¼ **cup chopped carrot**
 ¼ **cup chopped green *or* sweet red**
    pepper
 2 **cloves garlic, minced**
 1 **tablespoon olive oil *or* cooking oil**
 1 **28-ounce can tomatoes, cut up**
 1 **6-ounce can tomato paste**
 ¼ **cup dry red wine *or* water**
 1 **teaspoon dried Italian seasoning,**
    crushed
 ½ **teaspoon sugar**
 ¼ **teaspoon salt**
 ¼ **teaspoon dried thyme, crushed**
 ¼ **teaspoon pepper**
 1 **bay leaf**
	● For sauce, in a large saucepan cook mushrooms, onion, carrot, green *or* red pepper, and garlic in 1 tablespoon hot oil till tender. Stir in *undrained* tomatoes, tomato paste, wine or water, Italian seasoning, sugar, salt, thyme, pepper, and bay leaf. Bring to boiling; reduce heat. Cover and simmer for 30 minutes.

1 **beaten egg** ¼ **cup fine dry bread crumbs** ¼ **cup finely chopped onion** 3 **tablespoons grated Parmesan cheese** 2 **tablespoons milk *or* water** 2 **tablespoons snipped fresh parsley** ¼ **teaspoon salt** ¼ **teaspoon fennel seed, crushed** ¼ **teaspoon pepper** ¾ **pound ground beef *or* ground pork** 1 **tablespoon olive oil *or* cooking oil**	● For meatballs, combine egg, bread crumbs, onion, Parmesan cheese, milk or water, parsley, salt, fennel seed, and pepper. Add ground beef or pork; mix well. Shape into 32 meatballs. In a large skillet cook meatballs, half at a time, in 1 tablespoon hot oil about 8 minutes or till no pink remains, turning often. Drain fat.
4 **cups hot cooked spaghetti**	● Add meatballs to simmering sauce. Return to boiling; reduce heat. Simmer, uncovered, for 10 to 15 minutes or to desired consistency, stirring occasionally. Discard bay leaf. Serve over hot cooked spaghetti. Makes 4 servings.

Nutrition information per serving: 587 calories, 29 g protein, 68 g carbohydrate, 22 g fat (7 g saturated), 107 mg cholesterol, 803 mg sodium, 1,280 mg potassium.

Make It Easy ¾ **pound lean ground beef *or* pork**	Prepare Spaghetti and Meatballs as above, *except* omit meatballs and 1 tablespoon oil. Cook beef or pork with vegetables; drain fat.

Nutrition information per serving: 475 calories, 29 g protein, 62 g carbohydrate, 12 g fat (3 g saturated), 64 mg cholesterol, 547 mg sodium, 1,268 mg potassium.

31

Tacos

This Southwestern dish has been an American favorite ever since it crossed the border from Mexico. We use the same spicy filling for Burritos, too. (See recipe, below.)

8 taco shells

● Heat taco shells according to package directions.

¾ pound ground beef, ground turkey,
　　or bulk pork sausage
½ cup chopped onion
1 clove garlic, minced

● Meanwhile, for filling, in a large skillet cook the ground beef, ground turkey, or sausage; onion; and garlic till the meat is brown and the onion is tender. Drain off fat.

1 8-ounce can tomato sauce
1 4-ounce can diced green chili
　　peppers, drained
2 to 3 teaspoons chili powder
¼ teaspoon ground cumin

● Stir in tomato sauce, chili peppers, chili powder, and cumin. Bring to boiling; reduce heat. Simmer, uncovered, for 5 minutes.

1 small avocado, chopped (optional)
1½ cups shredded lettuce
1 cup shredded sharp cheddar *or*
　　Monterey Jack cheese (4 ounces)
½ cup taco sauce

● Fill *each* taco shell with about ¼ cup of the meat mixture. If desired, top *each* with avocado. Add lettuce, cheese, and taco sauce. Makes 4 servings.

Nutrition information per serving: 436 calories, 28 g protein, 30 g carbohydrate, 24 g fat (10 g saturated), 91 mg cholesterol, 1,142 mg sodium, 655 mg potassium.

Burritos
4 10-inch flour tortillas

Prepare Tacos as above, *except* omit the taco shells. Wrap the tortillas tightly in foil and heat in a 350° oven for 10 minutes. Spoon about ½ cup of the meat mixture onto *each* tortilla just below the center.

Fold bottom edge of each tortilla up and over filling, just till mixture is covered. Fold opposite sides of each tortilla in, just till they meet. Roll up tortillas from the bottom. Secure with wooden toothpicks, if necessary.

Arrange on a baking sheet. Bake in a 350° oven for 10 to 12 minutes or till heated through. Remove toothpicks. Serve on the shredded lettuce. If desired, sprinkle avocado on top. Top with cheese and taco sauce.

Nutrition information per serving: 486 calories, 30 g protein, 42 g carbohydrate, 23 g fat (10 g saturated), 91 mg cholesterol, 1,233 mg sodium, 662 mg potassium.

Chicken with Lemon Stuffing

7 cups dry bread cubes
½ cup finely chopped onion
2 teaspoons finely shredded lemon
    peel
½ teaspoon dried marjoram, crushed
½ teaspoon dried thyme, crushed
¼ teaspoon salt
1 clove garlic, minced
1 slightly beaten egg
½ cup margarine *or* butter, melted
3 tablespoons water
2 tablespoons lemon juice

● For stuffing, in a mixing bowl combine bread cubes, onion, lemon peel, marjoram, thyme, salt, garlic, and ¼ teaspoon *pepper.* Mix well.

In another mixing bowl combine *egg, melted margarine or butter, water, and lemon juice.* Drizzle over bread cube mixture, tossing lightly.

1 2½- to 3-pound broiler-fryer chicken

● Rinse chicken; pat dry. If desired, rub salt inside the body cavity. Spoon some of the stuffing loosely into the neck cavity; fasten the neck skin to the back with a small skewer. Lightly spoon stuffing into the body cavity. Tie the drumsticks securely to the tail. Twist the wing tips under the back. Put any remaining stuffing in a 1-quart casserole; chill.

1 tablespoon cooking oil, *or* margarine *or* butter, melted

● Place the chicken, breast side up, on a rack in a shallow roasting pan. Insert a meat thermometer into the center of an inside thigh muscle. Brush the chicken with cooking oil, melted margarine, or butter.

Roast, uncovered, in a 375° oven for 1¼ to 1½ hours or till no longer pink and the meat thermometer registers 180° to 185°.

Place the casserole with remaining stuffing in the oven with the chicken during the last 20 to 30 minutes of cooking. Remove chicken from the oven and cover with foil. Let stand 15 to 20 minutes before carving.

¼ cup all-purpose flour
Chicken broth *or* water

● Meanwhile, for gravy, after removing roasted chicken from pan, pour drippings into a large measuring cup. Also scrape the browned bits into the cup. Skim fat from pan juices, reserving ¼ cup fat. Reserve all the drippings.

In a saucepan combine reserved fat and flour. Add enough chicken broth to reserved drippings to measure 2 cups liquid. Add all at once to the flour mixture. Cook and stir till thickened and bubbly. Cook and stir 1 minute more. Makes 6 servings.

Nutrition information per serving: 606 calories, 29 g protein, 30 g carbohydrate, 40 g fat (10 g saturated), 118 mg cholesterol, 584 mg sodium, 298 mg potassium.

Crispy Fried Chicken

Pack this tried and true all-American favorite for your next picnic. Be sure to keep it thoroughly chilled until it's eaten.

1 cup all-purpose flour
1½ teaspoons dried basil, crushed
½ teaspoon salt
½ teaspoon onion powder
¼ teaspoon pepper
1 2½- to 3-pound broiler-fryer chicken, cut up
½ cup buttermilk

● In a plastic bag combine flour, basil, salt, onion powder, and pepper. Set aside.

Skin chicken, if desired. Rinse chicken; pat dry. Add chicken pieces, 2 or 3 pieces at a time, to plastic bag, shaking to coat well.

Dip chicken pieces, 1 at a time, into buttermilk. Add again to plastic bag with flour mixture, shaking to coat well.

2 tablespoons cooking oil

● Heat oil in a 12-inch skillet. Place the meaty pieces of chicken (breast halves, thighs, and large ends of drumsticks) toward the center of the skillet. Place remaining pieces toward edge.

Cook, uncovered, over medium heat for 15 minutes, turning to brown evenly. Reduce heat to medium-low and cook, uncovered, for 35 to 40 minutes more or till chicken is tender and no longer pink, turning occasionally. Remove chicken; drain on paper towels. Transfer chicken to a serving platter; keep warm.

2 tablespoons all-purpose flour
1 teaspoon instant chicken bouillon granules
⅛ teaspoon pepper
1¾ cups milk
Mashed Potatoes (see recipe, page 61) (optional)

● For the gravy, stir flour, bouillon granules, and pepper into drippings in the skillet, scraping up brown bits. Add milk all at once. Cook and stir over medium heat till thickened and bubbly. Cook and stir for 1 minute more. If desired, serve with Mashed Potatoes. Serves 6.

Nutrition information per serving: 376 calories, 29 g protein, 23 g carbohydrate, 18 g fat (5 g saturated), 82 mg cholesterol, 455 mg sodium, 372 mg potassium.

Making gravy is like making any other sauce. If you measure the ingredients correctly and follow the recipe, you'll get good results every time.

Stir the fat and flour together with a wooden spoon. Add the milk all at once; stir to mix well. Be sure to scrape up the crusty brown bits left on the bottom of the skillet by the fried chicken. These add flavor to the gravy.

Oven-Fried Chicken

**2 cups four-grain cereal flakes,
  coarsely crushed**
½ teaspoon onion salt
**⅛ teaspoon ground sage *or* ground
  ginger**
⅛ teaspoon pepper

● For coating mixture, on waxed paper or in a shallow dish combine cereal, onion salt, sage or ginger, and pepper. Set aside.

**2 to 2½ pounds meaty chicken pieces
  (breast halves, thighs, and
  drumsticks) *or* 1 pound boned
  skinless chicken breast halves**
**2 tablespoons melted margarine *or*
  butter**

● Skin chicken, if desired. Rinse chicken; pat dry. Brush chicken with melted margarine or butter. Roll chicken pieces in coating mixture. In a 15x10x1-inch or 13x9x2-inch baking pan arrange chicken pieces, skin side up, so pieces don't touch. Drizzle with any remaining margarine or butter and sprinkle with any remaining coating mixture.

   Bake in a 375° oven for 45 to 55 minutes for meaty chicken pieces or about 20 minutes for boned chicken breasts or till chicken is tender and no longer pink. Serves 4.

Nutrition information per serving: 352 calories, 29 g protein, 18 g carbohydrate, 18 g fat (4 g saturated), 89 mg cholesterol, 477 mg sodium, 270 mg potassium.

Grilling Basics

For a sizzling, not fizzling, fire, check out these barbecue pointers.
● Estimate the number of charcoal briquettes needed by spreading them into a single layer that extends about an inch beyond the size of the food to be cooked.
● Pile briquettes into a mound in the center of the grill. Drizzle liquid lighter or jelly fire starter over entire charcoal surface. Wait 1 minute; ignite with a match. Or, use an electric fire starter. Charcoal is ready when it's glowing or gray and has no black showing. This usually takes about 20 to 30 minutes.
● When the coals are ready, spread them according to the appropriate directions:
   For direct cooking: Spread the hot coals into a single layer with long-handled tongs. For more even heat and fewer flare-ups, arrange the coals ½ inch apart.
   For indirect cooking: Move coals from center of grill with long-handled tongs. Place a disposable foil drip pan in the center of the grill; arrange coals in a circle around the pan.
● Determine the temperature of the coals by holding your hand, palm side down, above the coals at the height your food will be cooked. Then start counting the seconds, "one thousand one, one thousand two." If you need to withdraw your hand after 2 seconds the coals are *hot;* after 3 seconds, *medium-hot;* after 4 seconds, *medium;* after 5 seconds, *medium-slow;* and after 6 seconds, *slow.*
● To reduce flare-ups, raise the grill rack, cover the grill, move the hot coals farther apart, or remove a few coals. As a last resort, remove the food from the grill and mist the fire with water from a pump-spray bottle.

JULY FOURTH CELEBRATION

*C*elebrate our country's independence by treating a group of friends to this purely American menu.

MENU

•

BARBECUED CHICKEN
(page 37)

COTTAGE CHEESE AND POTATO SALAD
(page 53)

PEACHY LEMONADE
(page 79)

WHITE CHOCOLATE AND NUT ICE CREAM
(page 84)

Menu Countdown

1 Day Ahead: Prepare and refrigerate the sauce for the *Barbecued Chicken*. Prepare and refrigerate the *Cottage Cheese and Potato Salad*. Prepare and

refrigerate the *Peachy Lemonade*.
4 to 6 Hours Ahead: Prepare the *White Chocolate and Nut Ice Cream*.
1¼ Hours Ahead: Start the coals.
1 Hour Ahead: Grill the *Barbecued Chicken*.

Barbecued Chicken

Awaken your tastebuds with this zippy tomato sauce slathered on grilled or broiled chicken.

2 to 2½ pounds meaty chicken pieces (breast halves, thighs, and drumsticks)

● If desired, skin chicken. Rinse; pat dry. If necessary, split breast pieces in half lengthwise.

½ cup catsup
¼ cup finely chopped onion
2 tablespoons brown sugar
1 tablespoon vinegar
1 tablespoon cooking oil
2 teaspoons Worcestershire sauce
½ teaspoon chili powder
½ teaspoon dry mustard
Few dashes bottled hot pepper sauce

● For sauce, in a small saucepan combine the catsup, onion, brown sugar, vinegar, oil, Worcestershire sauce, chili powder, dry mustard, and hot pepper sauce. Bring to boiling; reduce heat. Cover and simmer for 3 to 4 minutes or till onion is tender.

Place chicken, bone side up, on an uncovered grill directly over *medium* coals. Grill 20 minutes or till lightly browned. Turn chicken and grill 15 to 25 minutes or till tender and no longer pink, brushing occasionally with barbecue sauce during the last 10 minutes. Makes 4 servings.

Nutrition information per serving: 318 calories, 26 g protein, 17 g carbohydrate, 16 g fat (4 g saturated), 81 mg cholesterol, 473 mg sodium, 405 mg potassium.

Sweet-Sour Sauced Chicken
¼ cup pineapple preserves
2 tablespoons soy sauce

Prepare Barbecued Chicken as above, *except* reduce catsup to 2 tablespoons and omit Worcestershire sauce. Stir preserves and soy sauce into the barbecue sauce. Brush sauce on during the last 2 minutes of cooking only.

Nutrition information per serving: 350 calories, 26 g protein, 25 g carbohydrate, 16 g fat (4 g saturated), 81 mg cholesterol, 690 mg sodium, 328 mg potassium.

Oven Directions: Prepare Barbecued Chicken as above, *except* place chicken, skin side down, on the unheated rack of a broiler pan. Broil 4 to 5 inches from the heat about 20 minutes. Turn chicken, skin side up, and broil for 5 to 15 minutes more or till tender and no longer pink. During the last 5 minutes of cooking, brush occasionally with the barbecue sauce. Heat the remaining sauce; pass with chicken. Serve as above.

Chicken and Dumplings

1 2½- to 3-pound broiler-fryer chicken, cut up
3 cups water
1 medium onion, cut into wedges
1 teaspoon dried basil, crushed
½ teaspoon salt
¼ teaspoon dried marjoram, crushed
¼ teaspoon pepper
1 bay leaf
1 cup sliced celery
1 cup thinly sliced carrots
½ cup sliced fresh mushrooms

● Skin chicken, if desired. Rinse chicken. In a Dutch oven combine chicken, water, onion, basil, salt, marjoram, pepper, and bay leaf. Bring to boiling; reduce heat. Cover and simmer for 25 minutes. Add celery, carrots, and mushrooms. Return to boiling; reduce heat. Cover and simmer for 10 minutes more or till chicken and vegetables are tender. Discard the bay leaf.

1 cup all-purpose flour
1 tablespoon snipped fresh parsley
2 teaspoons baking powder
¼ teaspoon salt
¼ teaspoon dried oregano, crushed
1 beaten egg
¼ cup milk
2 tablespoons cooking oil

● For dumplings, in a bowl combine flour, parsley, baking powder, salt, and oregano.

In another bowl combine the egg, milk, and oil. Add to flour mixture. Stir with a fork just till moistened. Drop batter from a spoon onto the hot chicken pieces in the broth, making 6 dumplings *(do not drop batter into the liquid)*. Return to boiling; reduce heat. Cover and simmer for 10 to 12 minutes or till a wooden toothpick inserted into a dumpling comes out clean. *Do not lift cover while simmering.*

Transfer chicken, dumplings, and vegetables to a serving platter. Keep warm.

½ cup cold water
¼ cup all-purpose flour

● For gravy, pour broth into a large measuring cup. Skim fat from broth; discard fat. Measure *2 cups* of the broth; add to Dutch oven. Combine cold water and flour. Stir into the broth. Cook and stir till bubbly. Cook and stir 1 minute more. Serve gravy over chicken and vegetables with dumplings. Makes 6 servings.

Nutrition information per serving: 380 calories, 28 g protein, 26 g carbohydrate, 18 g fat (4 g saturated), 111 mg cholesterol, 484 mg sodium, 418 mg potassium.

Make It Easy
1¼ cups packaged biscuit mix

Prepare Chicken and Dumplings as above, *except* for dumplings omit the flour, baking powder, salt, and oil. In a mixing bowl stir together the biscuit mix, parsley, and oregano. In another mixing bowl stir together egg and milk. Add to dry mixture. Stir with a fork just till moistened. Continue as above.

Nutrition information per serving: 344 calories, 27 g protein, 21 g carbohydrate, 16 g fat (4 g saturated), 111 mg cholesterol, 590 mg sodium, 408 mg potassium.

Chicken and Cheese Potpies

As the television was added to many American homes, people looked to potpies as a portable dining option—the first television dinners!

Pastry for Single-Crust Pie (see recipe, page 92)

● Prepare pastry as directed. Roll out the pastry to ⅛-inch thickness; cut out four 5-inch circles. Cut scraps into decorative shapes. Cover and set aside.

1 **cup milk**
½ **cup chicken broth**
⅓ **cup all-purpose flour**
¼ **cup thinly sliced green onion**
  Dash pepper
2 **slices process Swiss cheese, torn into pieces (2 ounces)**
2 **teaspoons Dijon-style mustard *or* prepared mustard**

● In a large saucepan combine milk, chicken broth, flour, green onion, and pepper. Cook and stir till thickened and bubbly. Cook and stir for 1 minute more. Stir in the cheese and the mustard till the cheese is melted.

1 **10-ounce package frozen peas and carrots, thawed**
1¾ **cups chopped cooked chicken *or* turkey**
½ **cup chopped fully cooked ham**

● Stir in the peas and carrots, chicken or turkey, and ham. Cook and stir mixture till bubbly. Spoon hot mixture into four 10-ounce casseroles or custard cups.

1 **tablespoon milk**

● Place pastry circles over casseroles. Flute edges. Brush with milk. Top with decorative pastry cutouts. Brush with milk again. Cut slits in crust for steam to escape.

● Place potpies on a baking sheet. Bake in a 450° oven for 15 to 20 minutes or till the crust is golden brown. Makes 4 servings.

Nutrition information per serving: 520 calories, 36 g protein, 40 g carbohydrate, 25 g fat (8 g saturated), 79 mg cholesterol, 1,005 mg sodium, 527 mg potassium.

Make It Easy
½ **of one 15-ounce package folded refrigerated unbaked pie crusts (1 crust)**

Prepare Chicken and Cheese Potpies as above, *except* omit Pastry for Single-Crust Pie.

Trim the purchased pie crust to 2 inches larger than the diameter of a 1½-quart casserole. Pour the hot filling into the casserole. Top with the refrigerated pie crust. Flute edge. Brush with milk. Cut slits in top crust for steam to escape. Bake in a 450° oven about 25 minutes or till the crust is golden brown.

Chicken à la King

This American dish was created around the turn of the century at the Brighton Beach Hotel outside New York City. It wasn't inspired by royalty, but by Charles E. King II, the owner of the hotel. (Spinach Chicken à la King pictured opposite.)

1½ **cups loose-pack frozen mixed vegetables**
 1 **cup water**
 1 **tablespoon instant chicken bouillon granules**
 1 **tablespoon white wine Worcestershire sauce, dry white wine, *or* Worcestershire sauce**
 ½ **teaspoon dried basil, crushed**
 ⅛ **teaspoon pepper**

● In a large saucepan combine the frozen vegetables, water, bouillon granules, Worcestershire sauce or wine, basil, and pepper. Bring mixture to boiling; reduce heat. Cover and simmer for 5 minutes.

 2 **cups milk**
 ½ **cup all-purpose flour**
 2 **cups chopped cooked chicken *or* turkey**

● Meanwhile, combine milk and flour. Stir into vegetable mixture. Cook and stir till thickened and bubbly. Cook and stir 1 minute more. Stir in chicken or turkey; heat through.

 4 **frozen patty shells, baked according to package directions and tops removed**

● Serve the chicken mixture in the baked patty shells. Makes 4 servings.

Nutrition information per serving: 558 calories, 36 g protein, 51 g carbohydrate, 23 g fat (4 g saturated), 81 mg cholesterol, 1,056 mg sodium, 691 mg potassium.

 Spinach Chicken à la King
 ½ **of a 10-ounce package frozen chopped spinach, thawed and well drained**
 ¼ **teaspoon ground nutmeg**

Prepare Chicken à la King as above, *except* substitute spinach for the mixed vegetables and substitute nutmeg for the basil. Cook as above, *except* simmer for 2 minutes. Serve as above.

Nutrition information per serving: 528 calories, 35 g protein, 43 g carbohydrate, 23 g fat (4 g saturated), 81 mg cholesterol, 1,062 mg sodium, 675 mg potassium.

Chicken Noodle Soup

To duplicate the wonderful, full-flavored soup broth in the Make It Easy variation, we increased the amount of the chicken bouillon granules.

1 2½- to 3-pound broiler-fryer chicken, cut up
6 cups water
1 cup chopped onion
1 tablespoon instant chicken bouillon granules
1 tablespoon white wine Worcestershire sauce
1 teaspoon dried basil, crushed, *or* ¾ teaspoon dried dillweed
½ teaspoon salt
¼ teaspoon pepper
1 bay leaf

● If desired, skin the chicken. Rinse chicken. In a Dutch oven combine chicken, water, onion, bouillon granules, white wine Worcestershire sauce, basil or dillweed, salt, pepper, and bay leaf. Bring to boiling; reduce heat. Cover and simmer for 40 minutes. Remove the chicken from the pan.

● When chicken is cool enough to handle, remove meat from bones. Discard skin, if present, and bones. Chop chicken; set aside.

1½ cups chopped broccoli
¾ cup fine noodles
½ cup thinly sliced carrot

● Skim fat from cooking liquid. Add the broccoli, noodles, and carrot. Return to boiling; reduce heat. Cover and simmer for 8 to 10 minutes or till vegetables and noodles are tender. Discard the bay leaf. Stir in the chopped chicken; heat through. Serves 5.

Nutrition information per serving: 274 calories, 27 g protein, 11 g carbohydrate, 13 g fat (3 g saturated), 89 mg cholesterol, 882 mg sodium, 400 mg potassium.

Make It Easy
2 cups loose-pack frozen mixed vegetables *or* one 10-ounce package frozen mixed vegetables
2½ cups chopped cooked chicken *or* turkey

Prepare Chicken Noodle Soup as above, *except* omit the broiler-fryer chicken, onion, salt, broccoli, and carrot. Increase the chicken bouillon granules to 3 tablespoons.

Combine the frozen vegetables and bouillon granules with the water, white wine Worcestershire sauce, basil or dillweed, pepper, and bay leaf.

Bring to boiling; add the noodles. Cover and simmer for 8 to 10 minutes or till vegetables and noodles are tender. Discard bay leaf. Stir in chicken or turkey; heat through.

Nutrition information per serving: 204 calories, 26 g protein, 16 g carbohydrate, 4 g fat (1 g saturated), 68 mg cholesterol, 1,735 mg sodium, 322 mg potassium.

Lemon Chicken Salad

Brighten your lunch break with this cool, refreshing salad. For variety, spoon the salad mixture into four large pita bread rounds, split and lined with lettuce leaves.

2 cups chopped cooked chicken *or* turkey
½ cup sliced celery
⅓ cup shredded carrot
2 tablespoons thinly sliced green onion
½ cup mayonnaise *or* salad dressing
1 teaspoon finely shredded lemon peel
1 tablespoon lemon juice

● In a mixing bowl combine chicken, celery, carrot, and green onion.

For the dressing, in another mixing bowl stir together mayonnaise or salad dressing, lemon peel, and lemon juice. Stir into the chicken mixture. Cover and chill at least 1 hour.

1 cup seedless grapes, halved; one 8-ounce can pineapple tidbits, drained; *or* 1 cup strawberries, halved
Lettuce leaves
¼ cup slivered *or* sliced almonds, toasted

● To serve, stir in the grapes, pineapple, or strawberries. Divide chicken mixture among 4 lettuce-lined plates. Sprinkle with almonds. Makes 4 servings.

Nutrition information per serving: 407 calories, 24 g protein, 12 g carbohydrate, 30 g fat (5 g saturated), 75 mg cholesterol, 230 mg sodium, 436 mg potassium.

Curried Chicken Salad
2 tablespoons chutney, chopped
½ teaspoon curry powder

Prepare Chicken Salad as above, *except* omit lemon peel and lemon juice. Stir chutney and curry powder into mayonnaise or salad dressing. Use pineapple as the fruit option. Serve as above.

Nutrition information per serving: 434 calories, 24 g protein, 18 g carbohydrate, 30 g fat (5 g saturated), 75 mg cholesterol, 313 mg sodium, 434 mg potassium.

Quick-Cooking Chicken

When a recipe calls for cooked chicken, you can use canned or frozen cooked chicken. Remember 1 cup of chopped cooked chicken is about 5 ounces. To quickly cook your own chicken, place chicken breast halves in a large skillet with 1⅓ cups water. Bring to boiling; reduce heat. Cover and simmer for 18 to 20 minutes for breast halves with bones (12 to 14 minutes for boneless pieces) or till chicken is tender and no longer pink. Drain and cut chicken into cubes.

Lemon-Dill Baked Fish

Create a light, refreshing summertime meal with grilled fish and Fresh Fruit Salsa.

1 pound fresh *or* frozen fish fillets *or* steaks, (½ to ¾ inch thick)
Salt (optional)

● Thaw fish, if frozen. Arrange fish in a greased 12x7½x2-inch baking dish, turning under thin edges. If desired, sprinkle fish lightly with salt.

1 tablespoon margarine *or* butter, melted
1 tablespoon lemon juice
1 tablespoon snipped fresh dillweed *or* 1 teaspoon dried dillweed
⅛ teaspoon pepper

● In a mixing bowl combine the melted margarine or butter, lemon juice, dillweed, and pepper. Brush over fish.

Lemon slices

● Bake fish, uncovered, in a 450° oven for 6 to 12 minutes or till fish flakes easily with a fork. Garnish with lemon slices. Makes 4 servings.

Nutrition information per serving: 119 calories, 20 g protein, 1 g carbohydrate, 4 g fat (1 g saturated), 47 mg cholesterol, 100 mg sodium, 234 mg potassium.

Baked Fish with Fresh Fruit Salsa
½ of a small ripe papaya, peeled, seeded, and chopped
1 small ripe nectarine, pitted and chopped
1 fresh jalapeño chili pepper, seeded and chopped, *or* 1 tablespoon capers, drained
1 tablespoon snipped fresh rosemary, basil, *or* thyme, *or* 1 teaspoon dried rosemary, basil, *or* thyme, crushed
1 tablespoon olive oil *or* cooking oil

Prepare Lemon-Dill Baked Fish as above, *except* omit the lemon juice, dillweed, and pepper. In a bowl combine the papaya, nectarine, jalapeño pepper or capers, herb, and oil. Cover and chill thoroughly. Brush fish with butter and bake as directed. Omit the lemon slices. Serve with salsa.

Nutrition information per serving: 174 calories, 20 g protein, 7 g carbohydrate, 7 g fat (1 g saturated), 47 mg cholesterol, 132 mg sodium, 370 mg potassium.

Grill Directions: Prepare Lemon-Dill Baked Fish as above, *except* do not bake fish. Place fish in a well-greased grill basket. Brush with lemon mixture; close basket.

Grill on an uncovered grill directly over *medium-hot* coals 4 to 9 minutes or till fish flakes easily with a fork, turning once and brushing with lemon mixture.

Microwave Directions: Prepare Lemon-Dill Baked Fish as above, *except* place fish in a 12x7½x2-inch microwave-safe dish. Cover with vented clear plastic wrap. Micro-

cook on 100% power (high) for 7 to 9 minutes or till fish flakes easily with a fork, giving the dish a half-turn once. Serve as above.

Fish and Chips

Fish and baked potatoes originally were sold on the street corners of London. The baked potato soon was replaced by fried, sliced potatoes, or "chips," because they were easier to eat.

1 pound fresh *or* frozen fish fillets, cut ½ inch thick	● Thaw fish, if frozen. Cut into 3x2-inch pieces. Rinse and pat dry; set aside.
Cooking oil *or* shortening for deep-fat frying	● In a large deep saucepan or deep-fat fryer, heat 1½ to 2 inches of oil or shortening to 375°.
1 cup all-purpose flour **½ teaspoon baking powder** **¼ teaspoon salt** **¼ teaspoon ground black *or* red pepper** **⅛ teaspoon garlic powder** **1 cup beer *or* milk** **1 tablespoon cooking oil**	● Meanwhile, for batter, in a mixing bowl combine the flour, baking powder, salt, pepper, and garlic powder. Make a well in the center. Combine the beer or milk and the 1 tablespoon oil; add to dry ingredients. Beat mixture with a rotary beater till batter is nearly smooth.
	● Dip fish into batter, turning to coat. Fry fish, a few pieces at a time, in hot oil about 4 minutes or till fish is done and coating is golden brown, turning once. Using a slotted spoon, remove fish from oil. Drain on paper towels.
Crispy Baked Potato Wedges (see recipe, page 63) **Malt vinegar *or* cider vinegar (optional)**	● Keep cooked fish warm in a 300° oven while frying remaining fish. Serve with Crispy Baked Potato Wedges. If desired, pass malt or cider vinegar. Makes 4 servings.

Nutrition information per serving: 796 calories, 28 g protein, 78 g carbohydrate, 40 g fat (6 g saturated), 47 mg cholesterol, 510 mg sodium, 1,109 mg potassium.

Salmon Patties with Cheese Sauce

Add a splash of color to your dinner plate by nestling the salmon in a bed of steamed shredded zucchini. Then top with the cheese sauce.

1 beaten egg white
2 tablespoons milk
1 teaspoon dried minced onion
½ teaspoon dillweed
⅛ teaspoon pepper
1 7¾-ounce can salmon, drained, flaked, and skin and bones removed
½ cup finely crushed wheat crackers

● In a mixing bowl combine the egg white, milk, onion, dillweed, and pepper. Add salmon and crushed crackers; mix well. Form mixture into three ¾-inch-thick patties.

1 tablespoon cooking oil

● In a large skillet cook patties in hot oil over medium-low heat about 6 minutes or till coating is golden brown, turning once. Transfer to a serving platter; keep warm.

1 tablespoon margarine *or* butter
2 teaspoons all-purpose flour
Dash pepper
½ cup milk
½ cup shredded American cheese (2 ounces)

● For cheese sauce, in a small saucepan melt margarine or butter. Stir in flour and pepper. Add milk all at once. Cook and stir over medium heat till thickened and bubbly. Cook and stir 1 minute more. Stir in cheese till melted. Spoon sauce over patties. Serves 3.

Nutrition information per serving: 338 calories, 23 g protein, 11 g carbohydrate, 22 g fat (7 g saturated), 55 mg cholesterol, 823 mg sodium, 456 mg potassium.

Make It Easy
3 slices American cheese

Prepare Salmon Patties with Cheese Sauce as above, *except* omit the cheese sauce ingredients. Place the American cheese slices on the cooked patties in the skillet. Cover the skillet and remove from heat. Let stand for 2 to 3 minutes or till cheese melts. Or, if broiling patties, place the cheese slices atop patties during the last 15 seconds of broiling.

Nutrition information per serving: 312 calories, 24 g protein, 7 g carbohydrate, 21 g fat (8 g saturated), 60 mg cholesterol, 893 mg sodium, 404 mg potassium.

Broiler Directions: Prepare Salmon Patties with Cheese Sauce as above, *except* place patties in a greased shallow baking pan. Broil 3 to 4 inches from the heat for 5 to 6 minutes or till coating is lightly browned, turning once. Continue as above.

Tuna-Noodle Casserole

Americans turned to tuna as an economical, nutritious food source during World War I. The food that once fed our nation during a crisis maintains its popularity today.

4 ounces medium noodles *or* spinach noodles (3 cups)

● Cook the noodles according to the package directions. Drain and set aside.

1 cup chopped onion
¼ cup water
1 10¾-ounce can condensed cream of mushroom soup *or* cream of celery soup
1 5-ounce can (⅔ cup) evaporated milk *or* ⅔ cup milk
⅓ cup grated Parmesan cheese
1 tablespoon lemon juice

● Meanwhile, in a saucepan cook onion in water, covered, till tender. Drain. Stir in soup, milk, the ⅓ cup Parmesan cheese, and lemon juice.

1 6½-ounce can tuna, drained and broken into chunks
½ of an 8-ounce can water chestnuts, chopped, *or* ½ cup thinly sliced celery
1 2-ounce jar sliced pimiento, drained

● Gently stir in the tuna, water chestnuts or celery, pimiento, and the cooked noodles.

2 tablespoons grated Parmesan cheese

● Spoon into a 1½-quart casserole. Sprinkle with the 2 tablespoons Parmesan cheese.

● Bake, uncovered, in a 375° oven for 30 to 35 minutes or till heated through. Serves 4.

Nutrition information per serving: 362 calories, 24 g protein, 37 g carbohydrate, 13 g fat (5 g saturated), 85 mg cholesterol, 983 mg sodium, 484 mg potassium.

Vegetable Tuna-Noodle Casserole
2 cups loose-pack frozen broccoli, carrots, water chestnuts, and red peppers, thawed and drained

Prepare Tuna-Noodle Casserole as above, *except* omit milk, water chestnuts and pimiento. Stir in vegetables with tuna.

Nutrition information per serving: 326 calories, 22 g protein, 36 g carbohydrate, 10 g fat (3 g saturated), 75 mg cholesterol, 941 mg sodium, 325 mg potassium.

Tuna-Noodle Skillet

Prepare Tuna-Noodle Casserole as above, *except* omit spooning into the casserole. Heat the mixture through in a skillet, stirring gently.

Macaroni and Cheese

3 cups corkscrew macaroni (5 ounces)
¾ cup chopped green *or* sweet red pepper
¼ cup chopped onion
¼ cup water

● Cook pasta according to the package directions. Drain well.

In a large saucepan cook green or sweet red pepper and onion in water, uncovered, for 5 minutes or till tender. Drain.

1¾ cups milk
2 tablespoons flour
1 teaspoon white wine Worcestershire sauce *or* Worcestershire sauce
5 ounces American cheese, cubed

● Meanwhile, combine milk, flour, and Worcestershire sauce. Stir into vegetable mixture. Cook and stir till thickened and bubbly. Cook and stir for 1 minute more. Add American cheese; stir till melted. Stir in cooked pasta. Spoon mixture into a 1½-quart casserole.

1 cup cherry tomatoes, halved (optional)

● Bake, uncovered, in a 350° oven for 25 to 30 minutes or till bubbly, stirring gently after 15 minutes. If desired, stir in tomatoes. Makes 4 main-dish servings or 8 side-dish servings.

Nutrition information per serving: 347 calories, 17 g protein, 36 g carbohydrate, 15 g fat (8 g saturated), 100 mg cholesterol, 590 mg sodium, 370 mg potassium.

Make It Easy

Prepare Macaroni and Cheese as above, *except* decrease milk to 1½ cups. After stirring in the cooked macaroni, heat through. Do not bake. Serve immediately.

Nutrition information per serving: 340 calories, 17 g protein, 35 g carbohydrate, 15 g fat (8 g saturated), 98 mg cholesterol, 583 mg sodium, 346 mg potassium.

Dilled Macaroni and Cheese
5 ounces process Swiss cheese, torn
¼ teaspoon dried dillweed

Prepare Macaroni and Cheese as above, *except* substitute process Swiss cheese for the American cheese. Stir dillweed in with the milk.

Nutrition information per serving: 334 calories, 18 g protein, 36 g carbohydrate, 13 g fat (7 g saturated), 96 mg cholesterol, 568 mg sodium, 391 mg potassium.

Toasted Three-Cheese Sandwich

8 slices whole wheat bread, Texas toast bread, *or* other sliced bread

● Place bread on a baking sheet. Broil 3 to 5 inches from the heat for 1 to 2 minutes or till toasted. Turn and broil for 1 to 2 minutes more or till toasted.

½ cup soft-style cream-cheese (plain *or* flavored)
1 medium tomato, thinly sliced
½ of a small cucumber, thinly sliced
4 slices cheddar cheese (4 ounces)
4 slices brick, Monterey Jack, *or* mozzarella cheese (4 ounces)

● Spread *4 slices* of the bread with about *2 tablespoons* each of the cream cheese. Top with tomato and cucumber. Top with cheddar cheese slices and the brick, Monterey Jack, *or* mozzarella cheese slices.

Place cheese-topped bread on the baking sheet. Broil 3 to 5 inches from the heat for 1 to 2 minutes or till cheese is melted. Top with remaining bread. Makes 4 servings.

Nutrition information per serving: 469 calories, 22 g protein, 30 g carbohydrate, 30 g fat (17 g saturated), 87 mg cholesterol, 738 mg sodium, 277 mg potassium.

Egg Salad

10 hard-cooked eggs, chopped
¼ cup chopped celery
¼ cup finely chopped green *or* sweet red pepper
¼ cup mayonnaise *or* salad dressing
3 tablespoons sweet pickle relish
2 teaspoons prepared mustard
¼ teaspoon salt *or* seasoned salt
⅛ teaspoon pepper

● In a mixing bowl combine the eggs, celery, green or sweet red pepper, mayonnaise or salad dressing, pickle relish, mustard, salt or seasoned salt, and pepper. Cover and chill.

4 lettuce leaves
4 tomato slices

● To serve, stir egg mixture gently. Spoon over lettuce leaves. Garnish with tomato slices. Makes 4 servings.

Nutrition information per serving: 320 calories, 17 g protein, 8 g carbohydrate, 25 g fat (6 g saturated), 538 mg cholesterol, 490 mg sodium, 321 mg potassium.

Yogurt Egg Salad
2 tablespoons plain yogurt

Prepare Egg Salad as above, *except* decrease mayonnaise or salad dressing to 2 tablespoons. Add yogurt with mayonnaise.

Nutrition information per serving: 275 calories, 17 g protein, 9 g carbohydrate, 19 g fat (5 g saturated), 534 mg cholesterol, 456 mg sodium, 336 mg potassium.

ON THE SIDE

*P*ick from this savory sampler of side dishes to round out your meals. The chapter is filled with time-proven recipes including salads, soups, breads, and vegetables. And, each recipe is full of the fresh, natural tastes of homemade goodness.

Apple-Spinach Slaw and *Orange-Carrot Corn Sticks* are pictured at right. (See recipes, pages 52 and 72.)

Coleslaw

No one seems sure of the origins of coleslaw. What is certain is that there are many tasty variations of the robust cabbage salad, including Apple-Spinach Slaw. (See recipe, below. Pictured on page 51.)

¼ **cup mayonnaise *or* salad dressing**
¼ **cup plain yogurt *or* dairy sour cream**
1 **tablespoon vinegar**
1 **teaspoon sugar**
¼ **teaspoon dried dillweed *or* celery seed**
⅛ **teaspoon salt**
3 **cups coarsely shredded cabbage**
1 **cup shredded carrot**
½ **cup sliced radishes**
¼ **cup chopped onion**

● For the dressing, in a mixing bowl combine the mayonnaise or salad dressing, yogurt or sour cream, vinegar, sugar, dillweed or celery seed, and salt.

Toss with cabbage, carrot, radishes, and onion. Makes 4 to 6 servings.

Nutrition information per serving: 142 calories, 2 g protein, 10 g carbohydrate, 11 g fat (2 g saturated), 9 mg cholesterol, 177 mg sodium, 310 mg potassium.

Apple-Spinach Slaw
2 **tablespoons honey**
1 **tablespoon Dijon-style mustard**
1 **cup chopped apple**
1 **cup coarsely shredded fresh spinach**

Prepare Coleslaw as above, *except* omit the vinegar, sugar, dillweed or celery seed, carrot, and radishes. Decrease the cabbage to 2 cups.

Stir honey and mustard into mayonnaise-yogurt mixture. Stir chopped apple into the dressing. Toss the spinach with the cabbage and onion. Pour dressing atop and toss.

Nutrition information per serving: 188 calories, 3 g protein, 22 g carbohydrate, 12 g fat (2 g saturated), 9 mg cholesterol, 303 mg sodium, 384 mg potassium.

To shred the cabbage into long, coarse shreds, hold one-quarter of a head firmly against a cutting surface. Cut the cabbage into even shreds with a sharp knife.

Cottage Cheese and Potato Salad

Trim calories per serving by using low-fat cottage cheese and reduced-calorie mayonnaise or salad dressing. (Pictured on page 36.)

6 medium potatoes (about 2 pounds) *or* 2 pounds whole tiny new potatoes

● In a large saucepan cook potatoes, covered, in a small amount of lightly salted boiling water till just tender. (Allow 20 to 25 minutes for medium potatoes or 15 to 20 minutes for new potatoes.) Drain potatoes well. Peel and cube potatoes or quarter new potatoes.

**1 cup sliced celery
¾ cup chopped green *or* sweet red pepper
¼ cup finely chopped onion**

● In a mixing bowl combine celery, green or sweet red pepper, and onion. Add cooked potatoes. Toss to mix.

**1 cup cream-style cottage cheese
½ cup mayonnaise *or* salad dressing
2 tablespoons milk
1 tablespoon coarse-grain brown mustard *or* prepared mustard
½ teaspoon salt
½ teaspoon dried dillweed *or* basil, crushed, *or* celery seed (optional)
1 to 2 tablespoons milk (optional)**

● For dressing, in a blender container or food processor bowl combine cottage cheese, mayonnaise or salad dressing, 2 tablespoons milk, mustard, and salt. Cover and blend or process till mixture is smooth. Add to potato mixture. If desired, add dillweed, basil, or celery seed. Toss to combine all ingredients. Cover and chill at least 5 hours. If salad seems dry after chilling, stir in 1 to 2 tablespoons milk to moisten. Makes 8 to 10 servings.

Nutrition information per serving: 235 calories, 6 g protein, 26 g carbohydrate, 12 g fat (3 g saturated), 12 mg cholesterol, 362 mg sodium, 532 mg potassium.

**Herbed Potato Salad
1 tablespoon Italian dry salad dressing mix**

Prepare Cottage Cheese-Potato Salad as above, *except* omit the mustard, salt, and dillweed, basil, or celery seed. Add dry salad dressing mix to ingredients in blender or food processor. Continue as above.

Nutrition information per serving: 234 calories, 6 g protein, 26 g carbohydrate, 12 g fat (3 g saturated), 12 mg cholesterol, 226 mg sodium, 530 mg potassium.

Pasta Salad

When you're a little short on time, substitute ½ cup bottled clear Italian salad dressing for the dressing ingredients. (Pictured on page 8.)

1½ cups corkscrew macaroni *or* tricolor corkscrew macaroni

● Cook macaroni according to package directions; drain. Rinse with cold water; drain again.

½ of a small cucumber, halved lengthwise and thinly sliced (¾ cup)
1 small green pepper, cut into bite-size strips (¾ cup)
½ cup cubed cheddar cheese (2 ounces)
¼ cup chopped red onion
1 tablespoon snipped fresh parsley

● In a mixing bowl toss together the cooked macaroni, cucumber, green pepper, cheddar cheese, onion, and parsley.

¼ cup olive oil *or* salad oil
¼ cup grated Parmesan cheese
3 tablespoons red wine vinegar *or* lemon juice
2 teaspoons sugar
½ teaspoon dried basil, crushed
½ teaspoon dried oregano, crushed
¼ teaspoon garlic powder
¼ teaspoon pepper

● For dressing, in a screw-top jar combine the oil, Parmesan cheese, vinegar or lemon juice, sugar, basil, oregano, garlic powder, and pepper. Cover and shake well. Pour dressing over pasta mixture and toss lightly to coat. Cover and chill for 4 to 24 hours.

½ cup halved cherry tomatoes

● To serve, add the halved cherry tomatoes; gently toss salad. Makes 4 to 6 servings.

Nutrition information per serving: 384 calories, 12 g protein, 39 g carbohydrate, 21 g fat (6 g saturated), 19 mg cholesterol, 192 mg sodium, 164 mg potassium.

Creamy Pasta Salad
⅔ cup buttermilk salad dressing
½ cup mayonnaise *or* salad dressing
1 teaspoon dried dillweed

Prepare Pasta Salad as above, *except* omit the oil, Parmesan cheese, vinegar or lemon juice, sugar, basil, oregano, garlic powder, and pepper. Combine buttermilk salad dressing, mayonnaise or salad dressing, and dillweed. Pour dressing over the pasta mixture and toss gently. Continue as above.

Nutrition information per serving: 574 calories, 11 g protein, 39 g carbohydrate, 43 g fat (9 g saturated), 47 mg cholesterol, 425 mg sodium, 211 mg potassium.

Layered Vegetable Salad

4 cups torn mixed greens
1 cup cauliflower flowerets
2 small tomatoes, cut into thin wedges
2 hard-cooked eggs, sliced
1 cup shredded carrots
1 cup cubed mozzarella or Monterey
    Jack cheese (4 ounces)
1 cup loose-pack frozen peas

● Place the mixed greens in the bottom of a clear medium salad bowl. Layer the cauliflower, tomatoes, eggs, carrots, cheese, and frozen peas atop greens.

½ cup dairy sour cream or plain yogurt
½ cup creamy cucumber or buttermilk
    salad dressing

● For dressing, combine sour cream or yogurt and salad dressing. Spread evenly over salad, sealing to edges. Cover; chill up to 24 hours.

½ cup chopped avocado
½ cup alfalfa sprouts

● To serve, top with avocado and alfalfa sprouts. Makes 6 servings.

Nutrition information per serving: 295 calories, 11 g protein, 13 g carbohydrate, 23 g fat (5 g saturated), 90 mg cholesterol, 325 mg sodium, 487 mg potassium.

Spiced Peach Molds

1 8-ounce can peach slices (juice pack)
    or one 8¾-ounce can unpeeled
    apricot halves
    Peach or apricot nectar
    (about 1½ cups)
6 inches stick cinnamon
4 whole cloves

● Drain peaches or apricots, reserving juice. Add enough peach or apricot nectar to the reserved juice to make 2 cups liquid. Coarsely chop peaches or apricots; set aside.

In a medium saucepan combine *1 cup* of the juice-nectar mixture, the cinnamon, and cloves. Bring to boiling; reduce heat. Cover and simmer for 10 minutes. Remove from heat; remove cinnamon and cloves from liquid.

1 3-ounce package orange- or lemon-
    flavored gelatin

● Add gelatin to hot juice-nectar mixture in the saucepan, stirring till gelatin dissolves. Stir in remaining juice-nectar mixture. Transfer to a bowl. Chill 1 hour or till partially set (the consistency of unbeaten egg whites).

Fold in peach or apricot pieces. Pour into a 3- or 4-cup mold. (Or, pour into six ½-cup molds.) Cover; chill at least 4 hours or till firm.

Lettuce leaves

● Line a serving plate with lettuce. Dip mold into warm (not hot) water for a few seconds to loosen. Unmold onto plate. Serves 6.

Nutrition information per serving: 72 calories, 1 g protein, 18 g carbohydrate, 0 g fat, 0 mg cholesterol, 16 mg sodium, 111 mg potassium.

GRILLED VEGETABLE TIMINGS

Make supper simple by cooking both your meat and vegetables on the grill. Follow the directions below for precooking the vegetables. Then generously brush vegetables with melted margarine, butter, or olive oil for flavor and to prevent sticking. Cook directly over *medium-hot* coals till fork tender and slightly charred.

Vegetable	Preparation	Precooking time	Grilling time
Asparagus	Snap off and discard tough bases of stems. Precook; tie asparagus in bundles with strips of cooked green onion tops.	3 to 4 minutes	3 to 5 minutes
Fresh baby carrots	Cut off tops. Wash; peel.	3 to 5 minutes	3 to 5 minutes
Eggplant	Cut off top and blossom ends. Cut eggplant crosswise into 1-inch-thick slices.	Do not precook.	8 minutes
Sweet peppers	Remove stem. Quarter peppers. Discard seeds and membranes. Cut into 1-inch-wide strips.	Do not precook.	8 to 10 minutes
Leeks	Cut off green tops; trim bulb roots and remove 1 or 2 layers of white skin.	10 minutes or till tender. Halve lengthwise.	5 minutes
New potatoes	Halve potatoes.	10 minutes or till almost tender.	10 to 12 minutes
Zucchini	Wash; cut off ends. Quarter lengthwise into long strips.	Do not precook.	5 to 6 minutes
Scallopini squash	Rinse and trim ends.	Precook whole for 3 minutes.	20 minutes

Lemon-Almond Green Beans

¾ **pound fresh green beans *or* 3 cups loose-pack frozen cut *or* French-style green beans**

● If using fresh green beans, cut into 1-inch pieces or lengthwise slices. Cook, covered, in a small amount of boiling water till beans are crisp-tender. (Allow 20 to 25 minutes for 1-inch pieces or 10 to 12 minutes for lengthwise slices.) If using frozen green beans, cook according to package directions. Drain.

1 **cup sliced fresh mushrooms**
2 **tablespoons sliced green onion**
1 **tablespoon margarine *or* butter**
¼ **cup slivered almonds *or* chopped pecans, toasted**
1 **teaspoon finely shredded lemon peel**

● Meanwhile, for sauce, in a small saucepan cook mushrooms and green onion in margarine or butter till tender. Remove from heat. Stir in almonds and lemon peel. Toss with hot drained beans. Makes 4 servings.

Nutrition information per serving: 111 calories, 4 g protein, 10 g carbohydrate, 8 g fat (1 g saturated), 0 mg cholesterol, 38 mg sodium, 391 mg potassium.

Herb-Buttered Corn on the Cob

Summer gatherings and fresh ears of corn are perfect companions. Select your favorite way to cook the corn from the directions below.

4 fresh ears of corn

● Remove husks from the ears of corn; scrub with a stiff brush to remove the silks. Rinse; pat dry. Place each ear on a piece of heavy foil. Wrap each ear of corn securely.

● Bake corn in a 450° oven about 30 minutes or till tender.

¼ cup margarine *or* butter, softened
½ teaspoon dried savory *or* basil, crushed
¼ teaspoon onion powder
¼ teaspoon seasoned salt
¼ teaspoon finely shredded lemon peel (optional)
⅛ teaspoon pepper

● In a mixing bowl stir together margarine or butter, savory or basil, onion powder, seasoned salt, lemon peel (if desired), and pepper. Spread on cooked corn. Makes 4 servings.

Nutrition information per serving: 186 calories, 3 g protein, 20 g carbohydrate, 12 g fat (2 g saturated), 0 mg cholesterol, 224 mg sodium, 207 mg potassium.

Grill Directions: Prepare Herb-Buttered Corn on the Cob as above, *except* omit baking the corn. Grill the foil-wrapped corn on an uncovered grill directly over *hot* coals (see tip, page 35) for 15 to 18 minutes or till tender, turning frequently. Continue as above.

Range-Top Directions: Prepare Herb-Buttered Corn on the Cob as above, *except* omit wrapping the corn in foil and baking. Cook the ears of corn, covered, in a small amount of lightly salted boiling water (or, uncovered, in enough boiling water to cover) 5 to 7 minutes or till tender. Continue as above.

Microwave Directions: Prepare Herb-Buttered Corn on the Cob as above, *except* omit wrapping the corn in foil and baking. Wrap each ear of corn in waxed paper. Place on paper towels in the microwave. Micro-cook on 100% power (high) for 9 to 12 minutes or till tender. Continue as above.

57

Baked Beans Combo

¾ **cup chopped onion**
4 **slices bacon, cut up**

● In a large skillet cook onion and bacon till the bacon is crisp and the onion is tender, but not brown. Drain off fat.

1 **15-ounce can garbanzo beans *or* butter beans, drained**
1 **15-ounce can navy beans *or* great northern beans, drained**
1 **8-ounce can red kidney beans, drained**
1 **8-ounce can tomato sauce**
¼ **cup packed brown sugar**
2 **to 4 tablespoons honey**
1 **tablespoon Worcestershire sauce**
½ **teaspoon dry mustard**

● Stir in garbanzo beans or butter beans, navy beans or great northern beans, kidney beans, tomato sauce, brown sugar, honey, Worcestershire sauce, and dry mustard. Pour the mixture into a 1½-quart casserole.

● Bake, covered, in a 375° oven for 45 minutes. Uncover and stir. Bake, uncovered, for 10 to 20 minutes more or till of desired consistency. Makes 6 to 8 servings.

Nutrition information per serving: 285 calories, 13 g protein, 52 g carbohydrate, 4 g fat (1 g saturated), 4 mg cholesterol, 623 mg sodium, 648 mg potassium.

Sweet-and-Sour Baked Beans
½ **cup chopped green *or* sweet red pepper**
1 **tablespoon margarine *or* butter**
1 **15¼-ounce can pineapple chunks (juice pack), drained**
2 **tablespoons vinegar**
1 **tablespoon soy sauce**

Prepare Baked Beans Combo as above, *except* omit the bacon, Worcestershire sauce, and dry mustard. Cook onion and green pepper in margarine or butter till tender, but not brown.

Stir the pineapple chunks, vinegar, and soy sauce into the bean mixture before baking. Continue as above.

Nutrition information per serving: 332 calories, 12 g protein, 62 g carbohydrate, 6 g fat (1 g saturated), 0 mg cholesterol, 745 mg sodium, 728 mg potassium.

Onion Rings

¾ **cup all-purpose flour**
¼ **teaspoon baking soda**
¼ **teaspoon salt**
¾ **cup buttermilk**
1 **tablespoon cooking oil**

● For batter, in a mixing bowl combine the flour, baking soda, and salt. Add buttermilk and the 1 tablespoon oil. Beat till nearly smooth.

Cooking oil *or* shortening for deep-fat frying
3 **medium onions, sliced ¼ inch thick and separated into rings**
Salt (optional)

● In a deep-fat fryer or large heavy saucepan heat 1½-inches of oil or shortening to 375°. Dip onion rings into batter, allowing excess batter to drain off. Fry, a few at a time, in hot oil for 2 to 2½ minutes or till golden, turning once. Remove and drain on paper towels. Place onion rings on a baking pan and keep warm in a 300° oven while frying remaining onion rings. If desired, sprinkle with salt. Makes 4 servings.

Nutrition information per serving: 397 calories, 5 g protein, 25 g carbohydrate, 31 g fat (4 g saturated), 2 mg cholesterol, 235 mg sodium, 186 mg potassium.

Parmesan-Herb Onion Rings
¼ **cup grated Parmesan cheese**
½ **teaspoon dried basil *or* oregano, crushed**

Prepare Onion Rings as above, *except* omit sprinkling fried rings with salt. Combine the Parmesan cheese and basil or oregano. Sprinkle over warm onion rings.

Nutrition information per serving: 420 calories, 7 g protein, 25 g carbohydrate, 33 g fat (5 g saturated), 6 mg cholesterol, 196 mg sodium, 198 mg potassium.

Creamy Broccoli Bake

Serve this full-flavored vegetable dish with beef, pork, or poultry.

4 cups broccoli flowerets *or* one 16-ounce package frozen cut broccoli
¾ cup chopped green *or* sweet red pepper
½ cup chopped onion
½ cup shredded carrot

● In a large saucepan bring a small amount of lightly salted water to boiling. Add broccoli, green or sweet red pepper, onion, and carrot. Return mixture to boiling; reduce heat. Cover and simmer for 5 to 7 minutes or till the vegetables are crisp-tender. Drain; set aside.

2 tablespoons margarine *or* butter
2 tablespoons all-purpose flour
1 tablespoon Dijon-style mustard *or* prepared mustard
1 teaspoon Worcestershire sauce
⅛ teaspoon pepper
½ cup milk
1 3-ounce package cream cheese, cut up
½ cup dairy sour cream
⅓ cup slightly crushed herb-seasoned croutons

● Meanwhile, for sauce, in a medium saucepan melt margarine or butter. Stir in flour, mustard, Worcestershire sauce, and pepper. Add milk all at once to flour mixture. Cook and stir till thickened and bubbly. Cook and stir 1 minute more. Remove from heat. Stir in cream cheese till melted. Stir in sour cream and broccoli mixture. Spoon into a 1½-quart casserole. Sprinkle with the crushed croutons.

● Bake in a 375° oven for 20 to 25 minutes or till heated through. Makes 6 servings.

Nutrition information per serving: 184 calories, 5 g protein, 13 g carbohydrate, 14 g fat (7 g saturated), 26 mg cholesterol, 235 mg sodium, 348 mg potassium.

Blue Cheese-Broccoli Bake
¼ cup crumbled blue cheese (1 ounce)

Prepare Creamy Broccoli Bake as above, *except* omit the mustard, Worcestershire sauce, and cream cheese. After thickening the sauce, stir in the blue cheese till melted.

Nutrition information per serving: 146 calories, 5 g protein, 11 g carbohydrate, 10 g fat (4 g saturated), 14 mg cholesterol, 173 mg sodium, 343 mg potassium.

Mashed Potatoes

The secret to creamy smooth mashed potatoes is mashing them just till the lumps are gone. Be careful if you're using an electric mixer not to overbeat—the potatoes will be sticky.

1½ **pounds potatoes (4 or 5 medium)**
 3 **tablespoons margarine *or* butter**
 ¼ **teaspoon salt**
 ⅛ **teaspoon pepper**
 ¼ **to ⅓ cup milk *or* whipping cream**

● Peel and quarter potatoes. Cook, covered, in a small amount of lightly salted boiling water for 20 to 25 minutes or till tender. Drain. Mash with a potato masher or beat with an electric mixer on low speed till almost smooth. Add margarine or butter, salt, and pepper. Gradually beat in enough milk or whipping cream to make light and fluffy. Makes 5 or 6 servings.

Nutrition information per serving: 172 calories, 3 g protein, 25 g carbohydrate, 7 g fat (2 g saturated), 1 mg cholesterol, 199 mg sodium, 422 mg potassium.

Tangy Mashed Potatoes
 ¾ **cup dairy sour cream *or* plain yogurt**
    Snipped parsley

Prepare Mashed Potatoes as above, *except* reduce milk or whipping cream to 2 to 4 tablespoons. Stir sour cream or yogurt into potatoes with the margarine or butter. Spoon mixture into a greased 1-quart casserole. Cover with foil. Bake in a 350° oven for 10 to 15 minutes or till heated through. Garnish with snipped parsley. (Or, chill potatoes in casserole up to 24 hours. Bake, covered, in a 350° oven about 55 minutes or till heated through, stirring once. Garnish with snipped parsley.)

Nutrition information per serving: 243 calories, 3 g protein, 26 g carbohydrate, 14 g fat (6 g saturated), 16 mg cholesterol, 215 mg sodium, 466 mg potassium.

Lemon-Chive Mashed Potatoes
 2 **tablespoons snipped fresh chives**
 1 **teaspoon finely shredded lemon peel**
 1 **to 2 teaspoons lemon juice**

Prepare Mashed Potatoes as above, *except* add snipped chives, lemon peel, and lemon juice with margarine or butter.

Nutrition information per serving: 173 calories, 3 g protein, 25 g carbohydrate, 7 g fat (2 g saturated), 1 mg cholesterol, 199 mg sodium, 427 mg potassium.

Scalloped Potatoes

This thoroughly American side dish is a delicious accompaniment to roasted meat or chicken. Change it to a main dish by adding cheese and ham (see recipe, below).

½ **cup chopped onion**
1 **clove garlic, minced**
2 **tablespoons margarine *or* butter**
2 **tablespoons all-purpose flour**
½ **teaspoon prepared mustard**
¼ **teaspoon salt**
⅛ **teaspoon pepper**
1 **cup milk *or* light cream**

● For sauce, in a small saucepan cook onion and garlic in margarine or butter till tender, but not brown. Stir in flour, mustard, salt, and pepper. Add milk or light cream all at once. Cook and stir till thickened and bubbly. Cook and stir for 1 minute more. Set aside.

3 **medium potatoes**

● If desired, peel potatoes. Thinly slice potatoes. Place *half* of the sliced potatoes in a greased 1-quart casserole. Cover with *half* of the sauce. Repeat layers. Bake, covered, in a 350° oven for 40 minutes.

3 **tablespoons fine dry bread crumbs**
2 **tablespoons grated Parmesan cheese**
1 **tablespoon margarine *or* butter, melted**

● Meanwhile, combine bread crumbs, Parmesan cheese, and melted margarine or butter. Uncover casserole; sprinkle with crumb mixture. Bake about 30 minutes more or till potatoes are tender. Makes 4 side-dish servings.

Nutrition information per serving: 247 calories, 6 g protein, 32 g carbohydrate, 11 g fat (3 g saturated), 8 mg cholesterol, 360 mg sodium, 481 mg potassium.

Cheesy Scalloped Potatoes and Ham
½ **cup shredded American cheese (2 ounces)**
1 **cup cubed fully cooked ham**

Prepare Scalloped Potatoes as above, *except* stir cheese into thickened sauce till melted. Stir in ham. Layer potatoes and sauce in a 1½-quart casserole. Makes 3 main-dish servings.

Nutrition information per serving: 473 calories, 24 g protein, 43 g carbohydrate, 23 g fat (9 g saturated), 54 mg cholesterol, 1,369 mg sodium, 820 mg potassium.

Crispy Baked Potatoes

The Crispy Baked Potato Wedges are the "chips" in Fish and Chips (see recipe, page 45).

**4 medium baking potatoes
(6 to 8 ounces each)**

● Scrub potatoes thoroughly with a vegetable brush. Cut the potatoes in half lengthwise.

3 tablespoons margarine *or* butter, melted
½ teaspoon seasoned salt *or* garlic salt
⅛ to ¼ teaspoon pepper
½ cup dairy sour cream, sour cream dip with chives, *or* plain yogurt (optional)

● In a 13x9x2-inch baking pan, combine melted margarine or butter, seasoned salt or garlic salt, and pepper.

Place potatoes, cut side down, in margarine or butter mixture. Bake in the 450° oven for 25 to 30 minutes or till tender and cut side of potato is browned and crispy. Lift out with a spatula. If desired, serve with sour cream, sour cream dip, or yogurt. Makes 4 servings.

Nutrition information per serving: 297 calories, 5 g protein, 51 g carbohydrate, 9 g fat (2 g saturated), 0 mg cholesterol, 270 mg sodium, 849 mg potassium.

Crispy Baked Potato Wedges

Prepare Crispy Baked Potatoes as above, *except* after halving potatoes, cut each half lengthwise into 3 or 4 wedges. Place potatoes, cut side down, in melted margarine mixture in a 15x10x1-inch baking pan; turn each wedge over. Continue as above, turning potatoes once during baking.

Crispy Baked Sweet Potatoes
4 medium sweet potatoes (6 to 8 ounces each)
¼ cup packed brown sugar
¼ teaspoon ground cinnamon

Prepare Crispy Baked Potatoes as above, *except* substitute sweet potatoes for baking potatoes. Omit the seasoned salt or garlic salt and pepper. Continue as above. When potatoes are tender, turn them cut side up in pan. Sprinkle with brown sugar and cinnamon. Return to 450° oven about 5 minutes more or till brown sugar begins to bubble. Omit sour cream, sour cream dip, or yogurt.

Nutrition information per serving: 305 calories, 3 g protein, 55 g carbohydrate, 9 g fat (2 g saturated), 0 mg cholesterol, 124 mg sodium, 649 mg potassium.

Twice-Baked Potatoes

2 large baking potatoes
(10 to 12 ounces each)

● Scrub potatoes thoroughly with a brush. Pat dry. Prick with a fork. Bake in a 425° oven for 40 to 60 minutes or till tender.

Cut potatoes in half lengthwise. Gently scoop out potato, leaving a thin shell. Place the potato pulp in a small mixer bowl.

½ cup sour cream dip with toasted onion
¼ cup finely shredded cheddar cheese
¼ cup finely shredded zucchini
¼ cup finely shredded carrot
⅛ teaspoon salt
⅛ teaspoon white pepper *or* pepper
1 to 2 tablespoons milk (optional)

● With an electric mixer on low speed or a potato masher, beat or mash potato pulp. Add sour cream dip, cheese, zucchini, carrot, salt, and pepper; beat till smooth. (If necessary to reach desired consistency, stir in 1 to 2 tablespoons milk.)

Spoon mashed potato mixture into potato shells. Place in a 10x6x2-inch baking dish.

Bake in a 425° oven for 20 to 25 minutes or till lightly browned. Makes 4 servings.

Nutrition information per serving: 261 calories, 6 g protein, 41 g carbohydrate, 9 g fat (5 g saturated), 20 mg cholesterol, 140 mg sodium, 735 mg potassium.

Horseradish Twice-Baked Potatoes
½ cup dairy sour cream
1 to 2 teaspoons prepared horseradish

Prepare Twice-Baked Potatoes as above, *except* use sour cream for sour cream dip. Add horseradish with the sour cream.

Hashed Brown Potatoes

2 slices bacon

● Cook bacon till crisp; drain. Discard drippings. Finely crumble bacon; set aside.

3 medium potatoes (1 pound)
¼ cup finely chopped onion
¼ cup finely chopped green *or* sweet red pepper *or* 3 tablespoons canned chopped green chili peppers, drained
¼ teaspoon salt
⅛ teaspoon pepper
2 tablespoons cooking oil

● Peel and shred potatoes. Rinse and pat dry. Combine potatoes, onion, green or sweet red pepper or chili peppers, salt, and pepper. Heat oil in a large skillet. Pat potato mixture into the skillet.

Cover; cook over medium heat 10 minutes or till bottom is crisp. Cut into 4 wedges; loosen and turn. Cook about 10 minutes more or till golden (reduce heat if potatoes brown too quickly). Sprinkle with bacon. Serves 4.

Nutrition information per serving: 171 calories, 3 g protein, 22 g carbohydrate, 9 g fat (1 g saturated), 3 mg cholesterol, 189 mg sodium, 375 mg potassium.

Fresh Tomato Soup

Lime adds a refreshing twist to this favorite. Pair it with the Toasted Three-Cheese Sandwich (see recipe, page 49) for a classic combo.

3 medium tomatoes, peeled and quartered, *or* one 16-ounce can tomatoes
1½ cups water
½ cup chopped onion
½ cup chopped celery
½ of a 6-ounce can (⅓ cup) tomato paste
1 tablespoon snipped fresh parsley
2 teaspoons instant chicken bouillon granules
2 teaspoons lime juice *or* lemon juice
1 teaspoon sugar
Few dashes bottled hot pepper sauce

● If desired, seed the *fresh* tomatoes. In a large saucepan combine water, fresh tomatoes or *undrained* canned tomatoes, onion, celery, tomato paste, parsley, bouillon granules, lime or lemon juice, sugar, and hot pepper sauce. Bring to boiling; reduce heat. Cover and simmer about 20 minutes or till celery and onion are very tender.

Snipped fresh parsley (optional)

● Place *one-third* of the mixture in a blender container. Cover and blend till smooth. (Or, place *half* of the soup in a food processor bowl. Cover and process till smooth.) Repeat with the remaining mixture. Return all of the mixture to the saucepan; heat through. If desired, garnish with parsley. Makes 4 servings.

Nutrition information per serving: 56 calories, 2 g protein, 12 g carbohydrate, 1 g fat (0 g saturated), 0 mg cholesterol, 487 mg sodium, 485 mg potassium.

Gazpacho
1 cup chopped cucumber
½ cup chopped green pepper

Prepare Fresh Tomato Soup as above, *except* omit heating through after blending the mixture. Stir cucumber and green pepper into blended soup. Chill soup before serving.

Nutrition information per serving: 65 calories, 3 g protein, 14 g carbohydrate, 1 g fat (0 g saturated), 0 mg cholesterol, 489 mg sodium, 566 mg potassium.

Double-Corn Chowder

Whip up a steaming bowl of this hearty chowder. You can have it on the table in about 15 minutes. (Triple-Corn Chowder pictured opposite.)

1 10-ounce package frozen whole kernel corn
½ cup water
½ cup chopped green *or* sweet red pepper
¼ cup chopped onion
2 teaspoons instant chicken bouillon granules
⅛ teaspoon pepper

● In a large saucepan combine corn, water, green or sweet red pepper, onion, chicken bouillon granules, and pepper. Bring to boiling; reduce heat. Cover and simmer for 5 minutes or till corn is tender. *Do not drain.*

2 cups milk
3 tablespoons all-purpose flour
½ cup chopped sliced dried beef *or* ham
¼ cup corn nuts *or* coarsely broken corn chips (optional)

● Stir together milk and flour. Stir into corn mixture. Cook and stir till thickened and bubbly. Cook and stir for 1 minute more. Stir in dried beef. If desired, garnish each serving with corn nuts or chips. Makes 4 servings.

Nutrition information per serving: 175 calories, 11 g protein, 27 g carbohydrate, 3 g fat (2 g saturated), 34 mg cholesterol, 1,006 mg sodium, 395 mg potassium.

Triple-Corn Chowder
¼ cup cornmeal

Prepare Double-Corn Chowder as above, *except* substitute the cornmeal for the flour.

Nutrition information per serving: 185 calories, 12 g protein, 30 g carbohydrate, 3 g fat (2 g saturated), 34 mg cholesterol, 1,006 mg sodium, 403 mg potassium.

Mexican Corn Chowder
1 7½-ounce can tomatoes, cut up
3 tablespoons to ⅓ cup canned chopped green chili peppers, drained

Prepare Double-Corn Chowder as above, *except* reduce milk to ¾ cup and omit dried beef. Stir *undrained* tomatoes and chili peppers into the thickened mixture. Heat through.

Nutrition information per serving: 125 calories, 5 g protein, 26 g carbohydrate, 1 g fat (1 g saturated), 4 mg cholesterol, 629 mg sodium, 343 mg potassium.

French Onion Soup

Team a steaming bowl of this soup with a fresh spinach salad for a savorous light lunch.

2 cups thinly sliced onions
2 tablespoons margarine *or* butter
4 cups beef broth *or* chicken broth
**¼ cup dry red wine, beef broth, dry
   white wine, *or* chicken broth**
1 teaspoon Worcestershire sauce
⅛ teaspoon pepper

● In a large saucepan cook onions in margarine or butter for 10 to 15 minutes or till golden, stirring occasionally.

   Stir in 4 cups broth, ¼ cup wine or broth, Worcestershire sauce, and pepper. Bring mixture to boiling; reduce heat. Simmer, uncovered, for 10 minutes.

4 *or* 5 slices French bread, toasted
**¾ cup shredded Swiss *or* Gruyère
   cheese (3 ounces)**

● Meanwhile, sprinkle toasted bread with cheese. Place on a baking sheet. Broil 4 to 5 inches from the heat for 1 to 2 minutes or till cheese melts and turns light brown.

   To serve, ladle soup into bowls and float bread atop. Makes 4 or 5 side-dish servings.

Nutrition information per serving: 281 calories, 13 g protein, 24 g carbohydrate, 14 g fat (5 g saturated), 20 mg cholesterol, 1,124 mg sodium, 296 mg potassium.

Florentine Onion Soup
2 cups packed fresh spinach, chopped
**¼ cup grated Parmesan cheese
   (1 ounce)**

Prepare French Onion Soup as above, *except* omit the Swiss or Gruyère cheese and the toasting of the French bread.

   Cut bread into ¾-inch cubes. In a shallow pan, toast bread cubes in a 350° oven for 5 to 10 minutes or till toasted.

   Stir the spinach into the soup mixture after simmering; heat through. Pass the toasted bread cubes and the Parmesan cheese to sprinkle on each serving.

Nutrition information per serving: 230 calories, 10 g protein, 25 g carbohydrate, 9 g fat (3 g saturated), 5 mg cholesterol, 1,184 mg sodium, 434 mg potassium.

Herbed Potato Soup

Take your choice—hearty Herbed Potato Soup on a chilly winter day or refreshing Chilled Potato-Cucumber Soup on a warm summer day.

**2 cups cubed, peeled potato
(½-inch cubes)
1½ cups chicken broth
¼ cup thinly sliced green onion
1 teaspoon snipped fresh thyme *or*
basil *or* ¼ teaspoon dried thyme *or*
basil, crushed
⅛ teaspoon pepper**

● In a large saucepan combine potato, chicken broth, green onion, thyme or basil, and pepper.
Bring to boiling; reduce heat. Cover and simmer about 10 minutes or till cubed potatoes are tender. Slightly mash the cooked potatoes.

**½ cup plain yogurt
2 tablespoons all-purpose flour
1 cup milk
2 slices bacon, crisp-cooked, drained,
and crumbled**

● Meanwhile, combine yogurt and flour. Gradually stir in milk. Stir into potato mixture. Cook and stir till thickened and bubbly. Cook and stir for 1 minute more. Garnish each serving with bacon. Makes 5 side-dish servings.

Nutrition information per serving: 125 calories, 6 g protein, 18 g carbohydrate, 3 g fat (1 g saturated), 8 mg cholesterol, 317 mg sodium, 399 mg potassium.

**Buttermilk-Potato Soup
1½ cups buttermilk**

Prepare Herbed Potato Soup as above, *except* substitute buttermilk for the yogurt and milk. Increase the flour to 3 tablespoons.

Nutrition information per serving: 145 calories, 8 g protein, 21 g carbohydrate, 3 g fat (2 g saturated), 10 mg cholesterol, 378 mg sodium, 459 mg potassium.

**Chilled Potato-Cucumber Soup
2 teaspoons snipped fresh dillweed *or*
½ teaspoon dried dillweed
1 cup chopped, seeded cucumber
Thinly sliced cucumber, quartered
(optional)
Fresh dillweed (optional)**

Prepare Herbed Potato Soup as above, *except* substitute the dillweed for the thyme or basil and omit the bacon. Stir 1 cup chopped cucumber into thickened soup. Cover soup and chill thoroughly.
If desired, garnish the soup with thinly sliced cucumber and fresh dillweed.

Nutrition information per serving: 114 calories, 6 g protein, 19 g carbohydrate, 2 g fat (1 g saturated), 6 mg cholesterol, 279 mg sodium, 437 mg potassium.

MOVIE NIGHT

*E*njoy a casual soup supper while you watch your favorite movie. You can take it easy the night you serve this menu because everything is made ahead except the soup.

MENU

•

CREAMY CHEESE SOUP
(page 71)

MIXED GRAIN BREAD
(page 76)

DELI MEATS

CARAMEL CORN
(page 89)

Creamy Cheese Soup

Quickly soften the cream cheese in the microwave. Place the unwrapped cream cheese in a bowl. Heat, uncovered, on 100% power (high) for 15 to 30 seconds or till softened.

1½ **cups chicken broth**
¾ **cup coarsely shredded carrot**
¼ **cup sliced green onion**
1¼ **cups milk**
2 **tablespoons all-purpose flour**
½ **teaspoon dry mustard**
⅛ **teaspoon pepper**

● In a large saucepan combine chicken broth, carrot, and onion. Combine milk, flour, dry mustard, and pepper. Stir into chicken broth. Cook and stir over medium heat till thickened and bubbly. Cook and stir 1 minute more.

1 **3-ounce package cream cheese, cut into cubes and softened**
1 **cup shredded sharp cheddar or American cheese (4 ounces)**
1 **small tomato, peeled, seeded, and chopped**

● In a mixing bowl stir about *½ cup* of the hot broth mixture into cream cheese; stir till well blended. Stir cream cheese mixture into remaining broth mixture in saucepan. Stir cheddar or American cheese into mixture in saucepan till melted. Stir in tomato. Makes 4 side-dish servings.

Nutrition information per serving: 273 calories, 14 g protein, 12 g carbohydrate, 19 g fat (12 g saturated), 60 mg cholesterol, 578 mg sodium, 396 mg potassium.

Beer-Cheese Soup
½ **cup beer**
Small twisted pretzels

Prepare Creamy Cheese Soup as above, *except* reduce the chicken broth to 1 cup. Stir in beer with the chicken broth. Garnish each serving with a pretzel.

Nutrition information per serving: 304 calories, 14 g protein, 17 g carbohydrate, 19 g fat (12 g saturated), 60 mg cholesterol, 579 mg sodium, 384 mg potassium.

Honey Corn Bread

Enjoy this flavorful bread with soup or chili. (Orange-Carrot Corn Sticks pictured on page 50.)

1¼ cups cornmeal
¾ cup all-purpose flour
1 tablespoon baking powder
¼ teaspoon baking soda
¼ teaspoon salt
2 eggs
1 cup buttermilk *or* sour milk (see tip, page 101)
¼ cup honey *or* maple-flavored syrup
2 tablespoons margarine *or* butter, melted, *or* cooking oil

● In a mixing bowl stir together cornmeal, flour, baking powder, baking soda, and salt.

In another bowl beat together eggs, buttermilk, honey or syrup, and melted margarine, butter, or cooking oil. Add to cornmeal mixture and stir just till combined. *(Do not overbeat.)*

Pour into a greased 9x9x2-inch baking pan. Bake in a 425° oven about 20 minutes or till golden brown. Makes 9 servings.

Nutrition information per serving: 187 calories, 5 g protein, 32 g carbohydrate, 4 g fat (1 g saturated), 48 mg cholesterol, 256 mg sodium, 101 mg potassium.

Orange-Carrot Corn Bread
1 cup finely shredded carrot
½ teaspoon finely shredded orange peel

Prepare Honey Corn Bread as above, *except* stir carrot and orange peel into the cornmeal batter.

Nutrition information per serving: 194 calories, 5 g protein, 34 g carbohydrate, 4 g fat (1 g saturated), 48 mg cholesterol, 256 mg sodium, 144 mg potassium.

Corn Sticks

Prepare Honey Corn Bread or Orange-Carrot Corn Bread as above, *except* spoon batter into greased corn stick pans, filling pans ⅔ full. Bake in a 425° oven for 12 to 15 minutes or till golden brown. Makes about 24 six-inch sticks or 56 four-inch sticks.

Nutrition information per serving: 71 calories, 2 g protein, 12 g carbohydrate, 2 g fat (0 g saturated), 18 mg cholesterol, 94 mg sodium, 39 mg potassium.

Cheesy Mustard-Bacon Loaf

⅓ cup margarine *or* butter, softened
⅓ cup finely shredded Swiss cheese
¼ cup finely chopped green onion
2 slices bacon, crisp-cooked, drained, and crumbled *or* 2 tablespoons cooked bacon pieces
2 teaspoons Dijon-style mustard
2 teaspoons lemon juice
1 1-pound loaf French *or* Italian bread

● Combine softened margarine, cheese, green onion, bacon, mustard, and lemon juice.

Cut bread into 1-inch slices, cutting to, but not through, bottom of loaf. Spread *one side* of *each* slice with cheese mixture. Wrap in foil; place on a baking sheet. Bake in a 350° oven 20 to 25 minutes or till hot. Serves 16 to 18.

Nutrition information per serving: 130 calories, 4 g protein, 15 g carbohydrate, 6 g fat (2 g saturated), 3 mg cholesterol, 247 mg sodium, 39 mg potassium.

Banana-Nut Bread

Prevent ledges from forming on the edges of your bread by greasing the pan on the bottom and only ½ inch up the sides. The batter will cling to the pan sides instead of sliding down during baking.

1½ **cups all-purpose flour**
1½ **teaspoons baking powder**
 ¼ **teaspoon baking soda**
 ¼ **teaspoon ground allspice** *or* **nutmeg**
 ⅛ **teaspoon salt**

● In a large mixing bowl stir together the flour, baking powder, baking soda, allspice or nutmeg, and salt.

 1 **slightly beaten egg** *or* **2 egg whites**
 1 **cup mashed banana**
 ¾ **cup sugar**
 ¼ **cup cooking oil**
 1 **teaspoon finely shredded lemon peel (optional)**
 ½ **cup chopped walnuts** *or* **pecans**

● In another bowl combine egg or egg whites, banana, sugar, oil, and, if desired, lemon peel. Stir into flour mixture *just till moistened* (batter should be lumpy). Fold in nuts.

● Pour mixture into a greased 8x4x2-inch loaf pan. Bake in a 350° oven for 50 to 55 minutes or till a wooden toothpick inserted near the center comes out clean.

  Cool the bread in the pan for 10 minutes. Remove from pan and cool thoroughly on a wire rack. Wrap and store overnight before slicing. Makes 1 loaf (16 servings).

Nutrition information per serving: 151 calories, 2 g protein, 22 g carbohydrate, 6 g fat (1 g saturated), 13 mg cholesterol, 62 mg sodium, 92 mg potassium.

Banana-Java Bread
 2 **teaspoons instant coffee crystals**
 1 **tablespoon hot water**
 ½ **cup miniature semisweet chocolate pieces**

Prepare Banana-Nut Bread as above, *except* omit the allspice or nutmeg and lemon peel. Dissolve the coffee crystals in the hot water. Stir into the banana mixture with the oil. Fold chocolate pieces into the batter with the nuts.

Nutrition information per serving: 178 calories, 3 g protein, 26 g carbohydrate, 8 g fat (2 g saturated), 13 mg cholesterol, 62 mg sodium, 115 mg potassium.

Double-Swirl Apple Bread

5 to 5½ cups all-purpose flour
1 package active dry yeast
1 cup milk
3 tablespoons sugar
3 tablespoons margarine *or* butter
¾ teaspoon salt
2 eggs
1 cup shredded apple

● In a large mixer bowl combine *2 cups* of the flour and the yeast; set aside. In a saucepan heat and stir milk, sugar, margarine, and salt till warm (120° to 130°) and margarine almost melts. Add to flour mixture along with eggs and shredded apple. Beat with an electric mixer on low to medium speed 30 seconds, scraping the sides of the bowl constantly. Beat on high speed 3 minutes. Using a wooden spoon, stir in as much remaining flour as you can.

● Turn dough out onto a lightly floured surface. Knead in enough remaining flour to make a moderately stiff dough that is smooth and elastic (6 to 8 minutes total). Shape into a ball. Place in lightly greased bowl; turn once to grease surface. Cover; let rise in a warm place till double (about 60 minutes). Punch dough down. Turn out onto a lightly floured surface. Divide in half. Cover; let rest 10 minutes. Lightly grease two 9x5x3-inch loaf pans.

1½ cups finely chopped peeled apple
½ cup finely chopped walnuts *or* pecans, toasted
½ cup packed brown sugar
2 teaspoons ground cinnamon
2 tablespoons margarine *or* butter, softened

● Meanwhile, for filling, in a mixing bowl combine chopped apple, walnuts or pecans, brown sugar, and cinnamon. Set aside.
　Roll *half* of the dough to a 14x9-inch rectangle. Spread with *half* of the softened margarine; sprinkle with *half* of the filling.
　Beginning at both short ends, roll *each* end up, jelly-roll style, to center. Place loaf, rolled side up, in one loaf pan. Repeat with remaining dough, margarine or butter, and filling.

Powdered Sugar Glaze *or* powdered sugar

● Cover; let rise till almost double (about 30 minutes). Bake at 375° for 30 minutes or till bread sounds hollow when top is tapped with fingers. (If necessary, loosely cover with foil the last 15 minutes to prevent overbrowning). Remove from pans. Cool on wire racks. Drizzle with Powdered Sugar Glaze or sprinkle with powdered sugar. Makes 2 loaves (32 servings).

Nutrition information per serving: 140 calories, 3 g protein, 24 g carbohydrate, 4 g fat (1 g saturated), 14 mg cholesterol, 81 mg sodium, 74 mg potassium.

Powdered Sugar Glaze
¾ cup powdered sugar
¼ teaspoon vanilla
2 to 3 teaspoons milk

In a small bowl combine the powdered sugar and vanilla. Stir in enough of the milk to make a glaze of drizzling consistency.

Mixed Grain Bread

Blend cracked wheat, whole wheat flour, and rolled oats to make a hearty sandwich bread. (Pictured on page 70.)

2¾ to 3¼ cups all-purpose flour
½ cup cracked wheat
2 packages active dry yeast
1¾ cups milk
¼ cup packed brown sugar
3 tablespoons cooking oil
1 teaspoon salt

● In a large mixer bowl combine *2 cups* of the all-purpose flour, the cracked wheat, and yeast. Set aside.

In a medium saucepan combine milk, brown sugar, oil, and salt. Heat and stir over medium-low heat just till warm (120° to 130°). Add to flour mixture. Beat with an electric mixer on low speed for 30 seconds, scraping sides of bowl constantly. Beat on high for 3 minutes.

1½ cups whole wheat flour
½ cup rolled oats
Rolled oats

● Using a wooden spoon, stir in whole wheat flour, the ½ cup rolled oats, and as much of the remaining all-purpose flour as you can. Turn dough out onto a lightly floured surface. Knead in enough of the remaining all-purpose flour to make a moderately stiff dough that is smooth and elastic (6 to 8 minutes total). Shape into a ball. Place in a lightly greased bowl, turning once to grease surface of the dough. Cover; let rise in a warm place till double in size (about 1 hour).

● Punch dough down. Turn out onto a lightly floured surface. Divide in half. Cover and let rest 10 minutes. Lightly grease two 8x4x2-inch loaf pans. Shape *each* half into a loaf by patting or rolling. (To shape dough by patting, gently pull dough into a loaf shape, tucking edges beneath. To shape dough by rolling, on a lightly floured surface, roll each half into a 12x8-inch rectangle. Tightly roll up, jelly-roll style, starting from a short side. Seal with your fingertips as you roll.) Place in prepared pans.

Cover; let rise in a warm place till nearly double in size (about 30 to 45 minutes). Brush tops of loaves with water; sprinkle with the additional rolled oats.

● Bake in a 375° oven about 30 minutes or till bread sounds hollow when you tap the top with your fingers. (Cover loosely with foil the last 15 minutes of baking to prevent overbrowning, if necessary.) Immediately remove bread from pans. Cool on wire racks. Makes 2 loaves (32 servings).

Nutrition information per serving: 95 calories, 3 g protein, 17 g carbohydrate, 2 g fat (0 g saturated), 1 mg cholesterol, 75 mg sodium, 81 mg potassium.

Hot Cocoa Mix

Delight friends with a gift of this delicious mix.

1 3-quart-size package nonfat dry milk
    powder (3½ cups)
2 cups sifted powdered sugar
1 cup powdered nondairy creamer
½ cup sifted unsweetened cocoa
    powder

● In a mixing bowl combine dry milk powder, powdered sugar, nondairy creamer, and cocoa powder. Store in an airtight container.

For *each* serving, place ⅓ *cup* of the mix in a coffee cup or mug; add ¾ cup *boiling* water. Makes about 5½ cups mix (16 servings).

Nutrition information per serving: 141 calories, 6 g protein, 25 g carbohydrate, 3 g fat (2 g saturated), 3 mg cholesterol, 94 mg sodium, 333 mg potassium.

Buttermint Hot Cocoa Mix
¾ cup buttermints, crushed

Prepare Hot Cocoa Mix as above, *except* reduce powdered sugar to 1½ cups. Stir buttermints into mix with powdered sugar. Serve as above.

Nutrition information per serving: 152 calories, 6 g protein, 28 g carbohydrate, 3 g fat (2 g saturated), 3 mg cholesterol, 107 mg sodium, 333 mg potassium.

Mocha Mix
½ cup instant coffee crystals

Prepare Hot Cocoa Mix as above, *except* stir coffee crystals into mix. Serve as above.

Nutrition information per serving: 143 calories, 6 g protein, 26 g carbohydrate, 3 g fat (2 g saturated), 3 mg cholesterol, 95 mg sodium, 397 mg potassium.

Malted Hot Cocoa Mix
1 cup instant chocolate *or* vanilla
    malted milk powder

Prepare Hot Cocoa Mix as above, *except* stir malted milk powder into mix. Serve as above.

Nutrition information per serving: 177 calories, 7 g protein, 31 g carbohydrate, 3 g fat (3 g saturated), 4 mg cholesterol, 138 mg sodium, 400 mg potassium.

Spiced Apple Cider

Fill your kitchen with the wonderful aroma of this fall favorite.

3 cups apple cider *or* apple juice
¾ cup orange juice
¼ cup sugar
1 lemon, sliced
3 inches stick cinnamon
6 whole cloves
6 whole allspice
4 cardamom pods, opened (optional)

● In a medium saucepan combine the apple cider or apple juice, orange juice, sugar, lemon slices, cinnamon, cloves, allspice, and if desired, cardamom. Bring to boiling; reduce heat. Cover and simmer for 10 minutes. Strain the cider through a double thickness of 100% cotton cheesecloth. Discard lemon and spices. Serve warm. Makes 5 (6-ounce) servings.

Nutrition information per serving: 129 calories, 0 g protein, 33 g carbohydrate, 0 g fat, 0 mg cholesterol, 5 mg sodium, 271 mg potassium.

Spiced Rum Cider
1 to 2 tablespoons rum

Prepare Spiced Apple Cider as above, *except* stir in rum after straining.

Nutrition information per serving: 138 calories, 1 g protein, 33 g carbohydrate, 0 g fat, 0 mg cholesterol, 5 mg sodium, 271 mg potassium.

Java Jabber

Who can resist the penetrating aroma of freshly brewed coffee–especially first thing in the morning? Even those who aren't coffee drinkers often love the fresh aroma.

To make a good cup of coffee, fill a 10-cup coffee pot with *cold water* (about 7½ cups). Use ½ to ⅔ cup *ground coffee*. Brew the coffee according to the manufacturer's directions for your coffee maker.

You can add a special flavor to your coffee by adding one of the following to the ground coffee before you brew it.
● 1 tablespoon ground cinnamon
● 1 to 2 teaspoons almond extract
● ¼ cup unsweetened cocoa and 1 tablespoon sugar

Flavored coffee makes a nice gift, too. Mix the cinnamon or cocoa and sugar in the ground coffee and pour it into a decorative can or jar. Or, place it in a plastic bag; then put it in a decorative bag. Be sure to include the brewing directions.

Lemonade

Sip on one of three refreshing flavors of lemonade. (Peachy Lemonade pictured on page 36.)

3 cups cold water
1 cup lemon juice
¾ cup sugar
Ice cubes
Lemon slices

● In a 1½-quart pitcher stir together the water, lemon juice, and sugar till sugar is dissolved. If desired, chill. Serve over ice cubes. Garnish with lemon slices. Makes 4 (8-ounce) servings.

Nutrition information per serving: 159 calories, 0 g protein, 43 g carbohydrate, 0 g fat, 0 mg cholesterol, 1 mg sodium, 77 mg potassium.

Lemonade Floats
6 scoops orange, lime, lemon, *or* rainbow sherbet

Prepare Lemonade as above, *except* omit ice cubes. Place a scoop of sherbet in each of 6 tall glasses. Pour chilled lemonade over sherbet in glasses. If desired, stir to mix.

Nutrition information per serving: 196 calories, 1 g protein, 48 g carbohydrate, 1 g fat (1 g saturated), 5 mg cholesterol, 30 mg sodium, 117 mg potassium.

Peachy Lemonade
1 16-ounce can sliced peaches, chilled
Peach *or* nectarine slices (optional)

Prepare Lemonade as above, *except* place *half* of the *undrained* chilled peach slices in a blender or food processor container with *1 cup* of the lemonade. Cover; blend or process till smooth. Serve over ice. Repeat with remaining peaches and *1 cup* lemonade. (Refrigerate remaining lemonade for another use.) If desired, garnish with peach or nectarine slices.

Nutrition information per serving: 125 calories, 1 g protein, 33 g carbohydrate, 0 g fat, 0 mg cholesterol, 5 mg sodium, 171 mg potassium.

Use a citrus juicer when you need fresh citrus juice. First, cut the fruit in half. Then rotate the fruit on the juicer with a firm motion, squeezing the juice from the fruit. If necessary, pour the juice through a fine-mesh strainer to remove small seeds. To get the most juice, squeeze the fruit when it is at room temperature.

SWEET TREATS

*W*hen you're

looking for that just-right ending

to a wonderful meal, consider

some of our country's best from

the past. Homemade ice cream,

cakes, pies, and cookies all are

tempting choices. Peruse this

chapter's pages and reacquaint

yourself with many of the

scrumptious creations Americans

have loved for years.

Strawberry Shortcake is pictured

at right. (See recipe, page 82.)

Strawberry Shortcake

Strawberries are thought to have gotten their name from the way they originally were sent to market—strung on straw. Heap some luscious berries atop a flaky biscuit for a delightfully all-American dessert. (Make It Easy variation pictured on page 81.)

6 cups sliced strawberries
¼ cup sugar (optional)

● In a mixing bowl stir together strawberries and, if desired, the ¼ cup sugar. Set aside.

2 cups all-purpose flour
1 tablespoon baking powder
½ teaspoon cream of tartar
¼ teaspoon baking soda
½ cup margarine *or* butter
¾ cup buttermilk *or* sour milk

● In a mixing bowl combine the flour, baking powder, cream of tartar, and baking soda. Cut in the margarine or butter till mixture resembles coarse crumbs. Make a well in the center of this mixture; add the ¾ cup buttermilk all at once. Stir just till dough clings together.

1 tablespoon buttermilk *or* sour milk (optional)
1 teaspoon sugar (optional)

● On a lightly floured surface, knead dough gently for 10 to 12 strokes. *For individual shortcakes,* roll or pat dough to ½-inch thickness. Cut with a 2½- to 3-inch round biscuit cutter, dipping cutter into flour between cuts. Transfer biscuits to a baking sheet. If desired, brush with the 1 tablespoon buttermilk and sprinkle with the 1 teaspoon sugar. Bake in a 450° oven 10 to 12 minutes or till golden.
  For large shortcake, pat dough into an 8-inch circle on a baking sheet. Bake in a 450° oven for 12 to 15 minutes or till golden.

Cream Cheese Sauce *or* whipped cream

● Split shortcakes into 2 layers. Place bottom layers on serving plates or in bowls. Spoon some of the strawberries and the Cream Cheese Sauce on the bottom layers. Add top layers. Spoon more strawberries and Cream Cheese Sauce over the top. Pass any remaining berries. Serve immediately. Serves 10.

Nutrition information per serving: 272 calories, 5 g protein, 31 g carbohydrate, 14 g fat (4 g saturated), 10 mg cholesterol, 299 mg sodium, 224 mg potassium.

Cream Cheese Sauce
1 8-ounce carton dairy sour cream
1 3-ounce package cream cheese, softened
2 tablespoons sugar

In a mixing bowl stir together the sour cream, cream cheese, and sugar.

Make It Easy

Prepare Strawberry Shortcake as above, *except* increase the buttermilk in the dough to 1 cup. Drop dough from a tablespoon into 10 mounds on a greased baking sheet. Bake in a 450° oven for 10 to 12 minutes or till golden. Serve as above.

White Cheesecake

Decorate the top of the cheesecake by drizzling melted seedless raspberry preserves over each serving. (Pictured on page 102.)

1 cup rolled oats
¾ cup all-purpose flour
¼ cup packed brown sugar
½ cup margarine *or* butter
2 beaten egg yolks

● For crust, in a mixing bowl combine the oats, flour, and brown sugar. Cut in margarine or butter till crumbly. Set aside *¾ cup* of the mixture for the topping. Stir the egg yolks into the remaining mixture. Press onto the bottom and ½ inch up the sides of a 9-inch springform pan. Bake in a 375° oven for 8 minutes.

3 8-ounce packages cream cheese
½ cup sugar
2 tablespoons all-purpose flour
1 teaspoon vanilla
2 egg whites
1 cup whipping cream

● In a mixer bowl combine cream cheese, sugar, flour, and vanilla. Beat with an electric mixer till fluffy. Add egg whites all at once, beating on low speed just till combined. Stir in whipping cream. Pour into crust-lined pan. Sprinkle with reserved oat mixture.

● Place on a shallow baking pan in oven. Bake in a 375° oven for 40 to 45 minutes or till center appears nearly set when shaken. Cool 15 minutes. Loosen crust from pan sides. Cool 30 minutes more; remove sides of pan. Cool completely. Chill at least 4 hours. Makes 12 to 16 servings.

Nutrition information per serving: 455 calories, 8 g protein, 26 g carbohydrate, 36 g fat (19 g saturated), 125 mg cholesterol, 277 mg sodium, 147 mg potassium.

Orange Cheesecake
1 tablespoon orange liqueur
1 teaspoon finely shredded orange peel

Prepare White Cheesecake as above, *except* stir orange liqueur and orange peel in with the whipping cream.

Nutrition information per serving: 460 calories, 8 g protein, 27 g carbohydrate, 36 g fat (19 g saturated), 125 mg cholesterol, 277 mg sodium, 147 mg potassium.

Brown Sugar-Vanilla Ice Cream

Since the emergence of the ice-cream freezer in 1846, Americans have given homemade ice cream rave reviews. Select one of these outstanding flavors for your next get-together. (White Chocolate and Nut Ice Cream pictured on page 36.)

**2 cups half-and-half, light cream,
    or milk
1 cup packed brown sugar
2 beaten egg yolks**

● In a large saucepan combine half-and-half, light cream, or milk and brown sugar. Cook and stir over medium heat just till brown sugar dissolves. Stir about *1 cup* of the warm mixture into beaten egg yolks; return all to saucepan. Bring to boiling, stirring constantly. Reduce heat. Boil gently over medium-low heat for 2 minutes, stirring constantly.

**3 cups whipping cream
1 tablespoon vanilla
½ cup chopped pecans *or* almonds,
    toasted (optional)**

● Stir in the whipping cream and the vanilla. Cool. If desired, stir in pecans or almonds. Freeze in a 4- or 5-quart ice-cream freezer according to the manufacturer's directions. Makes 8 servings (about 2 quarts).

Nutrition information per serving: 504 calories, 4 g protein, 32 g carbohydrate, 41 g fat (25 g saturated), 198 mg cholesterol, 72 mg sodium, 244 mg potassium.

**White Chocolate and Nut Ice Cream
¾ cup sugar
4 ounces white baking bars *or* pieces
    with cocoa butter, melted
Sliced fresh strawberries,
    blueberries, *or* raspberries
    (optional)**

Prepare Brown Sugar-Vanilla Ice Cream as above, *except* omit the brown sugar and use almonds instead of pecans. In the saucepan combine half-and-half, light cream, or milk with the ¾ cup sugar. Cook as above, *except* stir the melted white baking bars into hot, cooked egg mixture, stirring till mixture is smooth (about 3 minutes). Continue as above. If desired, serve ice cream with fresh berries.

Nutrition information per serving: 554 calories, 5 g protein, 31 g carbohydrate, 46 g fat (28 g saturated), 198 mg cholesterol, 73 mg sodium, 190 mg potassium.

**Double Peanut Ice Cream
⅔ cup creamy peanut butter
½ cup chopped unsalted dry roasted
    peanuts
Hot fudge sauce (optional)**

Prepare Brown Sugar-Vanilla Ice Cream as above, *except* omit the pecans or almonds. Stir the peanut butter in with the *uncooked* egg yolk mixture. Cook as above. Stir the peanuts in just before freezing. If desired, serve with hot fudge sauce.

Nutrition information per serving: 683 calories, 12 g protein, 38 g carbohydrate, 57 g fat (28 g saturated), 198 mg cholesterol, 177 mg sodium, 466 mg potassium.

Banana Split Shake

For a classic trio, team a cool, creamy shake with a burger and fries.

1 ripe medium banana, peeled, sliced, and frozen
½ cup milk
2 tablespoons strawberry preserves
2 cups vanilla *or* chocolate ice cream *or* frozen yogurt

● In a blender container combine banana, milk, and preserves. Cover and blend till smooth. Add ice cream or yogurt. Cover and blend till smooth. Serve immediately in chilled glasses. Makes 2 (10-ounce) servings.

Nutrition information per serving: 406 calories, 8 g protein, 62 g carbohydrate, 16 g fat (9 g saturated), 65 mg cholesterol, 149 mg sodium, 595 mg potassium.

Peanut Butter-Banana Shake
2 tablespoons peanut butter
Chopped peanuts (optional)

Prepare Banana Split Shake as above, *except* substitute the peanut butter for the strawberry preserves. If desired, garnish with chopped peanuts.

Nutrition information per serving: 447 calories, 11 g protein, 51 g carbohydrate, 24 g fat (11 g saturated), 65 mg cholesterol, 224 mg sodium, 693 mg potassium.

Strawberry-Banana Yogurt Shake
1 8-ounce carton strawberry yogurt

Prepare Banana Split Shake as above, *except* reduce the milk to ¼ cup. Use the vanilla ice cream and reduce it to 1 cup. Add the strawberry yogurt to the blender container with the ice cream.

Nutrition information per serving: 372 calories, 9 g protein, 66 g carbohydrate, 9 g fat (5 g saturated), 37 mg cholesterol, 138 mg sodium, 640 mg potassium.

Cherry Cobbler

Choose between two different flavors for biscuit toppings. (Cinnamon-Corn Bread Cobbler pictured opposite.)

4 cups pitted tart red cherries *or* one 16-ounce package frozen unsweetened pitted tart red cherries
⅔ cup sugar
2 tablespoons cornstarch
2 tablespoons orange juice

● For filling, in a medium saucepan combine the cherries, the ⅔ cup sugar, cornstarch, and orange juice. Let fresh cherries stand for 10 minutes or let frozen cherries stand for 20 minutes. Cook and stir mixture over medium heat till thickened and bubbly. Cook and stir 1 minute more. Reduce heat and keep hot.

⅓ cup all-purpose flour
2 tablespoons finely crushed graham crackers
1 tablespoon finely chopped pecans
1 tablespoon brown sugar
¾ teaspoon baking powder
2 tablespoons margarine *or* butter

● Meanwhile, for biscuit topping, in a mixing bowl stir together the flour, crushed graham crackers, pecans, brown sugar, and baking powder. Cut in the margarine or butter till the mixture resembles coarse crumbs.

1 slightly beaten egg white
2 tablespoons milk
1½ teaspoons sugar
⅛ teaspoon ground cinnamon

● In a mixing bowl combine egg white and milk. Add all at once to the flour mixture, stirring just till moistened. Spoon the hot fruit mixture into a 10x6x2-inch baking dish. Immediately spoon the biscuit topping into 4 or 8 mounds atop the hot fruit mixture. Combine the 1½ teaspoons sugar and cinnamon. Sprinkle sugar mixture over the biscuit mounds.

Half-and-half, light cream, *or* vanilla ice cream (optional)

● Bake in a 400° oven for 12 to 15 minutes or till a wooden toothpick inserted into the center of a biscuit mound comes out clean. If desired, serve warm with half-and-half, light cream, or ice cream. Makes 4 servings.

Nutrition information per serving: 359 calories, 4 g protein, 71 g carbohydrate, 8 g fat (2 g saturated), 1 mg cholesterol, 166 mg sodium, 277 mg potassium.

Cinnamon-Corn Bread Cobbler
⅓ cup cornmeal
1 tablespoon sugar

Prepare the Cherry Cobbler as above, *except* for the topping, reduce the flour to 3 tablespoons and omit the graham crackers and brown sugar. Stir the cornmeal and the 1 tablespoon sugar in with the flour. Decrease the milk to 1 tablespoon. Continue as above.

Nutrition information per serving: 368 calories, 4 g protein, 73 g carbohydrate, 8 g fat (1 g saturated), 1 mg cholesterol, 142 mg sodium, 269 mg potassium.

Apple Crisp

Create a luscious sundae by serving the crisp over a scoop of vanilla or cinnamon ice cream.

5 cups sliced, peeled apples
¼ cup water
1 tablespoon lemon juice

● Place fruit in an 8x1½-inch round baking dish or a 10x6x2-inch baking dish. Combine water and lemon juice; pour over fruit in dish.

½ cup all-purpose flour
¼ cup packed brown sugar
½ teaspoon ground cinnamon
¼ cup margarine *or* butter

● For topping, in a mixing bowl combine flour, brown sugar, and cinnamon. Cut in margarine or butter till mixture resembles coarse crumbs. Sprinkle topping over fruit.

Vanilla ice cream, half-and-half, *or* light cream (optional)

● Bake, uncovered, in a 375° oven for 30 to 35 minutes or till fruit is tender and topping is golden. If desired, serve warm with ice cream, half-and-half, or light cream. Makes 6 servings.

Nutrition information per serving: 195 calories, 1 g protein, 30 g carbohydrate, 8 g fat (2 g saturated), 0 mg cholesterol, 94 mg sodium, 154 mg potassium.

Cranberry-Apple Crisp
1 cup coarsely chopped cranberries
¼ cup sugar

Prepare Apple Crisp as above, *except* add cranberries and ¼ cup sugar to apple mixture in baking dish.

Nutrition information per serving: 235 calories, 1 g protein, 41 g carbohydrate, 8 g fat (2 g saturated), 0 mg cholesterol, 95 mg sodium, 166 mg potassium.

Apple-Cookie Crunch
2 tablespoons sugar
¾ cup finely crushed vanilla wafers *or* crisp oatmeal cookies
¼ cup chopped pecans *or* almonds

Prepare Apple Crisp as above, *except* omit flour, brown sugar, and cinnamon. Reduce the margarine or butter to 3 tablespoons; melt the margarine or butter. Toss the apple mixture in the baking dish with the sugar. In a mixing bowl stir together crushed wafers or cookies, nuts, and the melted margarine or butter. Sprinkle over apples. Bake and serve as above.

Nutrition information per serving: 204 calories, 1 g protein, 26 g carbohydrate, 11 g fat (2 g saturated), 7 mg cholesterol, 108 mg sodium, 142 mg potassium.

Caramel Corn

Mix up a batch of this crunchy snack in a snap. (Pictured on page 70.)

7 to 8 cups popped popcorn **2 cups peanuts (optional)**	● Put the popcorn and, if desired, the peanuts into a 17x12x2-inch baking pan. Remove any unpopped kernels of popcorn.
¾ cup packed brown sugar **6 tablespoons margarine *or* butter** **3 tablespoons light corn syrup**	● In a medium saucepan combine the brown sugar, margarine or butter, and corn syrup.
	● Cook and stir mixture with a wooden spoon over medium heat till mixture boils. Cook without stirring for 5 minutes more. (Mixture should bubble gently over the entire surface.) Remove mixture from the heat.
¼ teaspoon baking soda **¼ teaspoon vanilla**	● Stir in the baking soda and vanilla. Pour mixture over popcorn, stirring to coat.
	● Bake in a 300° oven for 15 minutes. Stir mixture and bake 5 minutes more. Spread caramel corn on a large piece of buttered foil to cool. Makes 7 to 8 cups (7 servings).

Nutrition information per serving: 230 calories, 1 g protein, 35 g carbohydrate, 10 g fat (2 g saturated), 0 mg cholesterol, 159 mg sodium, 108 mg potassium.

Begin timing the 5-minute boiling period when the mixture bubbles at a moderate, steady rate over the entire surface.

Chocolate-Peanut Butter Fudge

Two yummy flavors in one creamy-smooth candy. (Pictured on page 102.)

2 cups sugar
½ cup milk
¼ cup creamy peanut butter
**2 squares (2 ounces) unsweetened
    chocolate, cut up**
2 tablespoons light corn syrup
2 tablespoons margarine *or* butter
1 teaspoon vanilla
**¾ cup chopped macadamia nuts,
    chopped peanuts, *or* chopped
    pecans (optional)**

● Line an 8x8x2-inch baking pan with foil, extending foil over the edges of the pan. Butter the foil; set prepared pan aside.

Butter the sides of a heavy 2-quart saucepan. In saucepan combine sugar, milk, peanut butter, chocolate, and corn syrup. Cook over medium-high heat to boiling, stirring constantly with a wooden spoon to dissolve sugar (about 5 minutes). Avoid splashing mixture on pan sides. Clip a candy thermometer to side of pan.

Cook over medium-low heat, stirring frequently, till thermometer registers 234°, soft-ball stage. (Mixture should boil at a moderate, steady rate over entire surface.) Reaching soft-ball stage should take 8 to 10 minutes. Remove pan from heat. Add margarine and vanilla; *do not stir.* Cool, without stirring, to 110° (about 55 minutes). Remove thermometer.

Beat vigorously with a wooden spoon till mixture just begins to thicken. If desired, add nuts. Beat till very thick and fudge just starts to lose its gloss (about 7 minutes total). Quickly pour into pan. While warm, score into sixty-four 1-inch squares; cool. When fudge is firm, lift out of pan; cut into squares. Makes 64 servings.

Nutrition information per serving: 52 calories, 1 g protein, 7 g carbohydrate, 3 g fat (1 g saturated), 0 mg cholesterol, 11 mg sodium, 24 mg potassium.

The fudge will be thin and very glossy when you begin beating. Beat with a wooden spoon till fudge just begins to thicken (see photo). Stir in the nuts.

Watch closely and continue beating the fudge till it becomes very thick and *just starts* to lose its gloss. At this point, *quickly* turn fudge into prepared pan.

Pumpkin Apple-Butter Pie

Pastry for Single-Crust Pie (see recipe, page 92)

● Prepare pastry as directed. Set aside.

½ of a 16-ounce can (1 cup) pumpkin
1 cup apple butter
⅓ cup packed brown sugar
½ teaspoon ground cinnamon
¼ teaspoon salt
¼ teaspoon ground nutmeg
3 slightly beaten eggs
1 5-ounce can (⅔ cup) evaporated milk

● In a mixing bowl combine pumpkin, apple butter, brown sugar, cinnamon, salt, and nutmeg. With a fork, lightly beat eggs into pumpkin mixture. Stir in evaporated milk. Pour into unbaked pastry shell. To prevent overbrowning, cover edge of pie with foil.

Whipped cream (optional)

● Bake in a 375° oven 25 minutes. Remove foil; continue baking 25 minutes more or till a knife inserted off center comes out clean. Cool on a wire rack. Cover and chill to store. If desired, serve with whipped cream. Serves 8.

Nutrition information per serving: 309 calories, 6 g protein, 45 g carbohydrate, 12 g fat (4 g saturated), 85 mg cholesterol, 182 mg sodium, 281 mg potassium.

Pecan Pie

Create a chocolate delight by reducing the pecans to 1 cup and adding ½ cup semi-sweet chocolate pieces to the pie with the pecans.

Pastry for Single-Crust Pie (see recipe, page 92)

● Prepare pastry as directed. Set aside.

3 slightly beaten eggs
1¼ cups light *or* dark corn syrup
½ cup packed brown sugar *or* sugar
2 tablespoons margarine *or* butter, melted
1 teaspoon vanilla
1½ cups pecan halves *or* coarsely chopped pecans

● In a mixing bowl combine eggs, corn syrup, sugar, margarine, and vanilla. Stir in pecans.

Place the pastry-lined pie plate on the oven rack. Pour the pecan mixture into the pie plate. Cover edge of pie with foil. Bake in a 350° oven for 25 minutes.

Remove foil; bake for 20 to 25 minutes more or till a knife inserted near the center comes out clean. Cool pie on a wire rack. Cover and chill to store. Makes 8 servings.

Nutrition information per serving: 542 calories, 6 g protein, 71 g carbohydrate, 29 g fat (5 g saturated), 80 mg cholesterol, 153 mg sodium, 188 mg potassium.

Walnut and Spice Pie
1 teaspoon ground cinnamon
¼ teaspoon ground nutmeg

Prepare Pecan Pie as above, *except* substitute walnuts for the pecans. Stir the cinnamon and nutmeg in with the walnuts.

Pastry for Single-Crust Pie

1¼ cups all-purpose flour
¼ teaspoon salt
⅓ cup shortening *or* lard

● In a mixing bowl stir together the flour and the salt. Cut in the shortening or lard till pieces are the size of small peas.

3 to 4 tablespoons cold water

● Sprinkle *1 tablespoon* of the water over part of the flour mixture; gently toss with a fork. Push to the side of the bowl. Repeat till all is moistened. Form dough into a ball.

● On a lightly floured surface, flatten dough with your hands. Roll dough from center to edges, forming a circle about 12 inches in diameter. Wrap pastry around rolling pin. Unroll onto a 9-inch pie plate. Ease pastry into pie plate, being careful not to stretch pastry.

Trim to ½ inch beyond edge of pie plate; fold under extra pastry. Make a fluted, rope-shape, or scalloped edge. *Do not prick pastry.* Bake as directed in individual recipes.

Use a pastry blender to cut the shortening into the flour till all of the mixture resembles small peas (as shown). If you don't have a pastry blender, you can use two knives in a crisscross motion to cut in the shortening.

Sprinkle *1 tablespoon* cold water over part of the flour mixture; gently toss with a fork. Push to the side of the bowl. Repeat just till all of the flour mixture is evenly moistened.

The pastry should be stiff, but not crumbly. If too much water is used, the pastry will be tough and may shrink; if too little is used, it will be crumbly.

Apple Pie with Cider Sauce

Apple pie came to America with the Pilgrims as a breakfast dish. Today, it's Americans' number-one favorite pie. (Pictured on page 8.)

Pastry for Double-Crust Pie

● Prepare pastry; set aside.

⅔ to ¾ cup sugar
1 tablespoon all-purpose flour
½ teaspoon ground cinnamon
⅛ teaspoon ground nutmeg
7 cups thinly sliced, peeled apples
1 cup dried mixed fruit bits, raisins, *or* dried cherries (optional)

● Combine the ⅔ to ¾ cup sugar, the flour, cinnamon, and nutmeg. Add the apples; toss to coat. If desired, sprinkle dried fruit evenly over bottom of the pastry-lined pie plate. Top with apple mixture. Cut slits in top crust. Adjust top crust; trim to ½ inch beyond edge of pie plate. Seal and flute edge.

---

1 beaten egg white
1 tablespoon water
2 teaspoons sugar
  Ice cream (optional)
  Cider Sauce (optional)

● Combine egg white and water; brush mixture over top crust. Sprinkle with the 2 teaspoons sugar. Cover edge of pie with foil. Bake in a 375° oven for 25 minutes. Remove foil. Bake 20 to 25 minutes more or till top is golden and fruit is tender. If desired, serve with ice cream and/or warm Cider Sauce. Serves 8.

Nutrition information per serving: 397 calories, 4 g protein, 56 g carbohydrate, 18 g fat (4 g saturated), 0 mg cholesterol, 142 mg sodium, 151 mg potassium.

Pastry for Double-Crust Pie
2 cups all-purpose flour
½ teaspoon salt
⅔ cup shortening *or* lard
6 to 7 tablespoons cold water

Stir together flour and salt. Cut in shortening till pieces are the size of small peas. Sprinkle *1 tablespoon* of the water over part of the flour mixture; gently toss with a fork. Push to side of bowl. Repeat till all is moistened. Divide dough in half. Form each half into a ball.

On a lightly floured surface, flatten a ball of dough with your hands. Roll dough from center to edges, forming a circle about 12 inches in diameter. Wrap pastry around rolling pin. Unroll into a 9-inch pie plate. Ease pastry into pie plate, being careful not to stretch pastry. Trim bottom pastry even with rim of pie plate.

For the top crust, roll the remaining dough half into a 12-inch circle.

Cider Sauce
2 cups apple cider *or* apple juice
6 inches stick cinnamon
2 tablespoons margarine *or* butter
2 tablespoons honey
1 tablespoon cornstarch

In a medium saucepan combine the apple cider or juice and the stick cinnamon. Bring to boiling; reduce heat. Simmer, uncovered, about 20 minutes or till liquid is reduced to *1 cup.* Strain through a sieve or colander lined with 100% cotton cheesecloth. Discard cinnamon. In the saucepan melt margarine or butter; stir in honey and cornstarch. Stir in the cider mixture. Cook and stir till thickened and bubbly. Cook and stir for 2 minutes more. Serve warm.

93

Angel Food Cake

Zero fat plus zero cholesterol equals one heavenly dessert. Try it with fresh fruit, too. (Confetti Angel Food Cake pictured on page 22.)

1½ **cups egg whites (10 to 12 large)**
1½ **cups sifted powdered sugar**
1 **cup sifted cake flour *or* sifted all-purpose flour**

● In a very large mixer bowl bring egg whites to room temperature. Meanwhile, sift powdered sugar and flour together 3 times. Set flour mixture aside.

1½ **teaspoons cream of tartar**
1 **teaspoon vanilla**
1 **cup sugar**

● Add cream of tartar and vanilla to egg whites. Beat with an electric mixer on medium to high speed till soft peaks form (tips curl). Gradually add sugar, about *2 tablespoons* at a time, beating on medium to high speed till stiff peaks form (tips stand straight).

Powdered Sugar Icing (optional)

● Sift about *one-fourth* of the flour mixture over beaten egg whites; fold in gently. (If bowl is too full, transfer to a larger bowl.) Repeat, folding in remaining flour mixture, using one-fourth of the flour mixture each time.

Gently pour into an *ungreased* 10-inch tube pan. Gently cut through the batter with a knife or a narrow metal spatula.

Bake on the lowest rack in a 350° oven for 40 to 45 minutes or till top springs back when lightly touched. *Immediately* invert cake in pan and cool thoroughly. Using a narrow metal spatula, loosen sides of cake from pan; remove cake. If desired, drizzle with Powdered Sugar Icing. Makes 12 servings.

Nutrition information per serving: 157 calories, 4 g protein, 36 g carbohydrate, 0 g fat, 0 mg cholesterol, 77 mg sodium, 67 mg potassium.

Powdered Sugar Icing
1 **cup sifted powdered sugar**
2 **to 3 tablespoons milk**
1 **to 2 drops red food coloring (optional)**

In a mixing bowl stir together sifted powdered sugar and enough milk to make an icing of drizzling consistency. If desired, stir in red food coloring. Drizzle over the top of the cake.

Confetti Angel Food Cake
2 **tablespoons tiny multi-colored decorative candies**

Prepare Angel Food Cake as above, *except* fold the decorative candies in with the last fourth of the flour mixture.

Coffee Angel Food Cake
2 **teaspoons instant coffee crystals**
2 **tablespoons unsweetened cocoa powder (optional)**

Prepare Angel Food Cake as above, *except* combine instant coffee crystals with vanilla. Stir to dissolve. Add to egg whites before beating. Continue as above. If desired, for Powdered Sugar Icing, stir cocoa powder into powdered sugar before adding milk. Omit food coloring.

Sour Cream-Chocolate Cake

1¾ cups all-purpose flour
 1 teaspoon baking powder
 ½ teaspoon baking soda
 ¼ teaspoon salt

● Grease and lightly flour two 9x1½-inch round baking pans. Stir together flour, baking powder, baking soda, and salt. Set aside.

 ½ cup shortening
1½ cups sugar
 ½ teaspoon vanilla
 2 eggs
 1 8-ounce carton dairy sour cream
 3 squares (3 ounces) unsweetened chocolate, melted and cooled
 1 cup water
   Sour Cream-Chocolate Frosting

● In a large mixer bowl beat shortening with an electric mixer on medium speed about 30 seconds or till softened. Add sugar and vanilla and beat till thoroughly combined. Add eggs, one at a time, beating 1 minute after each. Beat in ½ cup of the sour cream and cooled chocolate till combined. (Reserve remaining sour cream for frosting.) Add flour mixture and water alternately to beaten mixture, beating on low speed after each addition *just till combined.*

Pour batter into the prepared pans. Bake in a 350° oven for 30 to 35 minutes or till a wooden toothpick inserted near the center comes out clean. Cool cakes in pans on wire racks for 10 minutes. Remove from pans. Cool completely. Frost with Sour Cream-Chocolate Frosting. Chill to store. Serves 12.

Nutrition information per serving: 523 calories, 6 g protein, 73 g carbohydrate, 26 g fat (11 g saturated), 44 mg cholesterol, 171 mg sodium, 200 mg potassium.

Sour Cream-Chocolate Frosting
 4 squares (4 ounces) unsweetened chocolate, cut up
 ¼ cup margarine *or* butter
 1 tablespoon milk
 1 teaspoon vanilla
3½ to 4 cups sifted powdered sugar

In a saucepan combine the unsweetened chocolate and the margarine. Heat over low heat till melted, stirring frequently. Cool slightly. Stir in the remaining sour cream (⅓ cup), the milk, and vanilla. Gradually add the powdered sugar, beating by hand till frosting is smooth and reaches spreading consistency.

To successfully frost a layer cake, follow these easy steps. Brush loose crumbs from the sides of each layer. Arrange strips of waxed paper around the edge of a serving plate. Place the first cake layer, top side down, on the plate. Spread about *one-fourth* of the frosting over the top of this layer. Place the second cake layer, top side up, atop first layer. Be sure edges of cake align. Spread sides of cake with a thin coat of frosting. Spread a thick layer of frosting over this thin coat, swirling frosting decoratively. Spread remaining frosting over the cake top. Remove waxed paper strips from under cake.

Carrot Cake

2½ **cups all-purpose flour**
1½ **teaspoons baking powder**
1 **teaspoon baking soda**
1 **teaspoon ground cinnamon**
¼ **teaspoon ground allspice**
⅛ **teaspoon ground nutmeg**

● Grease and lightly flour two 9x1½-inch round baking pans. In a mixing bowl combine the flour, baking powder, baking soda, cinnamon, allspice, and nutmeg. Set mixture aside.

1 **cup margarine *or* butter**
1½ **cups packed brown sugar**
4 **eggs**
2 **teaspoons finely shredded orange peel (set aside)**
¼ **cup orange juice**
2½ **cups finely shredded carrots**
¾ **cup chopped walnuts**

● In a large mixer bowl beat the margarine or butter with an electric mixer on medium speed for 30 seconds. Add the brown sugar and beat till fluffy. Add the eggs, one at a time, beating well after each addition. Add the flour mixture and the orange juice alternately to the beaten mixture, beating on low speed after each addition *just till combined.* Stir in the carrots, walnuts, and orange peel.

● Pour batter into prepared pans. Bake in a 350° oven for 35 to 40 minutes or till a wooden toothpick inserted near the center comes out clean. Cool cakes in the pans on wire racks for 10 minutes. Remove cakes from pans. Cool thoroughly on wire racks.

Cream Cheese Frosting
1 **tablespoon powdered sugar**

● Meanwhile, prepare Cream Cheese Frosting. When cool, place one of the cake layers on a serving plate. Spread *one-third* of the frosting on top of the layer on the plate. Top with the remaining layer, its top side up. Use remaining frosting to frost sides of cake.

For a decorative top, arrange 2 cake racks, one on top of the other, so the rungs form diamond shapes. Lightly place on top of cake. Sift powdered sugar over the top. Carefully remove the racks. Or, use an 8-inch decorative paper doily instead of the cake racks. Store cake in refrigerator. Makes 12 servings.

Nutrition information per serving: 618 calories, 7 g protein, 83 g carbohydrate, 30 g fat (7 g saturated), 81 mg cholesterol, 412 mg sodium, 291 mg potassium.

Cream Cheese Frosting
½ **of an 8-ounce package cream cheese**
⅓ **cup margarine *or* butter**
1 **teaspoon vanilla**
3¾ **to 4 cups sifted powdered sugar**
1 **teaspoon finely shredded orange peel**

In a small mixer bowl beat together cream cheese, margarine or butter, and vanilla till light and fluffy. Gradually add about *half* of the powdered sugar, beating well. Gradually beat in enough of the remaining powdered sugar to make a frosting of spreading consistency. Stir in the finely shredded orange peel.

Lemon-Buttermilk Pound Cake

1 **cup margarine *or* butter**
6 **eggs**
1 **cup buttermilk *or* sour milk**
3 **cups all-purpose flour**
½ **teaspoon baking soda**

● Bring margarine or butter, eggs, and buttermilk to room temperature. Grease and flour a 10-inch fluted tube pan or two 8x4x2-inch loaf pans. In a mixing bowl stir together flour and baking soda. Set aside.

2¼ **cups sugar**
2 **teaspoons finely shredded lemon peel *or* orange peel (set aside)**
1 **tablespoon lemon juice *or* orange juice**
1 **teaspoon vanilla**
   Lemon Icing

● Beat margarine with an electric mixer on medium speed for 30 seconds. Gradually add sugar to margarine, about *2 tablespoons* at a time, beating on medium to high speed about 6 minutes total or till very light and fluffy. Add eggs, one at a time, beating 1 minute after each addition and scraping bowl frequently. Add lemon juice and vanilla; beat well. Gradually add flour mixture and buttermilk alternately to beaten mixture, beating on low to medium speed after each addition *just till combined.* Stir in lemon peel. Pour batter into prepared pan(s).

Bake in a 325° oven till a wooden toothpick inserted near center comes out clean (60 to 65 minutes for tube pan or 65 to 70 minutes for loaf pans). Cool on a wire rack 15 minutes. Remove from pan(s). Cool completely on a wire rack. Drizzle with Lemon Icing. Serves 18.

Nutrition information per serving: 315 calories, 5 g protein, 47 g carbohydrate, 12 g fat (3 g saturated), 72 mg cholesterol, 177 mg sodium, 72 mg potassium.

Lemon Icing
1 **cup sifted powdered sugar**
1 **teaspoon finely shredded lemon peel *or* orange peel**
3 **to 4 teaspoons lemon *or* orange juice**

In a mixing bowl stir together the powdered sugar, shredded lemon or orange peel, and enough lemon or orange juice to make an icing of drizzling consistency.

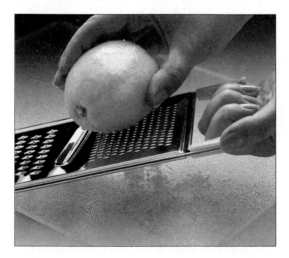

When a recipe calls for finely shredded lemon, orange, or lime peel, rub the fruit's rind across a very fine shredding surface to get the desired amount of peel. Shred only the outer layer of rind, since the inner white layer is very bitter.

To make the shredding easier, make sure the fruit's rind is dry and the fruit is at room temperature. If you have leftover shredded peel, seal, label, and freeze it for another use.

Black Walnut-Spice Cake

1 cup all-purpose flour
¾ cup sugar
1 teaspoon ground cinnamon
½ teaspoon baking powder
½ teaspoon baking soda
¼ teaspoon ground allspice
⅛ teaspoon salt
½ cup buttermilk *or* sour milk
¼ cup margarine *or* butter, softened
1 egg
¼ teaspoon vanilla
½ cup chopped black walnuts
    Maple Cream Cheese Glaze

● Combine the first 7 ingredients. Add buttermilk, margarine, egg, and vanilla. Beat with an electric mixer on low speed till combined. Beat on high speed 2 minutes. Stir in walnuts. Pour into a greased 8x8x2-inch baking pan. Bake in a 350° oven 25 to 30 minutes or till done. Cool cake in pan. Top with Maple-Cream Cheese Glaze. Store in refrigerator. Makes 9 to 12 servings.

Nutrition information per serving: 292 calories, 5 g protein, 44 g carbohydrate, 12 g fat (3 g saturated), 29 mg cholesterol, 188 mg sodium, 91 mg potassium.

Maple-Cream Cheese Glaze
½ of a 3-ounce package cream cheese, softened
2 teaspoons maple-flavored syrup
¼ teaspoon vanilla
1¼ cups sifted powdered sugar
1 to 2 teaspoons milk

In a small mixer bowl beat together the cream cheese, maple-flavored syrup, and vanilla till fluffy. Gradually add the powdered sugar, beating well. Beat in enough milk to make a mixture of glazing consistency.

Brownies

1 cup sugar
½ cup margarine *or* butter
⅓ cup unsweetened cocoa powder
2 eggs
1 teaspoon vanilla
⅔ cup all-purpose flour
½ teaspoon baking powder
¼ teaspoon salt
½ cup chopped walnuts
    Cocoa Glaze

● In a medium saucepan combine sugar, margarine, and cocoa powder. Cook and stir over medium heat till margarine melts. Remove from heat; cool 5 minutes. Add eggs and vanilla. Beat lightly by hand *just till combined.* Stir in flour, baking powder, and salt. Stir in walnuts. Spread batter in a greased 9x9x2-inch baking pan. Bake in a 350° oven for 25 minutes or till done. Cool completely.
    Frost with Cocoa Glaze. Makes 12 servings.

Nutrition information per serving: 260 calories, 3 g protein, 33 g carbohydrate, 14 g fat (3 g saturated), 36 mg cholesterol, 180 mg sodium, 87 mg potassium.

Cocoa Glaze
1 cup sifted powdered sugar
2 tablespoons unsweetened cocoa powder
2 tablespoons margarine *or* butter, softened
¼ teaspooon vanilla

In a mixing bowl combine powdered sugar and cocoa powder. Beat in margarine or butter, vanilla, and enough *boiling water* (1 to 2 tablespoons) to make a smooth glaze.

Chocolate Chip Cookies

If you prefer to use margarine in your cookies, select one that is not a spread, diet, or soft-style margarine product. Your cookies will not turn out satisfactorily with these products.

1 **cup margarine** *or* **butter**
2½ **cups all-purpose flour**
1 **cup sugar**
½ **cup packed brown sugar**
2 **eggs**
1 **teaspoon baking soda**
1 **teaspoon vanilla**
1 **12-ounce package (2 cups) semisweet chocolate pieces,** *or* **2 cups coarsely chopped white baking bars (or pieces) with cocoa butter** *or* **vanilla-flavored confectioner's coating**
¾ **cup chopped nuts (optional)**

● Beat margarine with an electric mixer on medium to high speed for 30 seconds. Add about *half* of the flour, the sugar, brown sugar, eggs, baking soda, and vanilla. Beat till thoroughly combined. Beat or stir in remaining flour. Stir in chocolate pieces and nuts.

Drop dough by rounded teaspoons 3 inches apart onto an ungreased cookie sheet. Bake in a 375° oven for 8 to 10 minutes or till edges are lightly browned. Remove and cool on a wire rack. Makes 48 cookies.

Nutrition information per cookie: 121 calories, 1 g protein, 15 g carbohydrate, 7 g fat (2 g saturated), 9 mg cholesterol, 67 mg sodium, 44 mg potassium.

Gingersnaps

¾ **cup margarine** *or* **butter**
2¼ **cups all-purpose flour**
1 **cup sugar**
¼ **cup molasses** *or* **honey**
1 **egg**
1 **teaspoon baking soda**
1 **teaspoon ground ginger**
1 **teaspoon ground cinnamon**
¼ **teaspoon ground mace** *or* **nutmeg**
⅓ **cup sugar**

● In large mixer bowl beat margarine or butter with electric mixer on medium to high speed for 30 seconds. Add about *half* of the flour, the 1 cup sugar, the molasses or honey, egg, baking soda, ginger, cinnamon, and mace or nutmeg. Beat till thoroughly combined. Beat or stir in remaining flour.

Shape dough into 1-inch balls. Roll balls in the ⅓ cup sugar. Place 2 inches apart on an ungreased cookie sheet. Bake in a 375° oven for 10 to 12 minutes or till set and tops are crackled. Remove cookies from baking sheet; cool on a wire rack. Makes 48 cookies.

Nutrition information per cookie: 70 calories, 1 g protein, 10 g carbohydrate, 3 g fat (1 g saturated), 4 mg cholesterol, 52 mg sodium, 25 mg potassium.

Chocolate Crisps
½ **cup packed brown sugar**
3 **squares (3 ounces) unsweetened chocolate, melted and cooled**
1 **teaspoon vanilla**

Prepare Gingersnaps as above, *except* omit the molasses or honey, ginger, cinnamon, and mace. Add brown sugar, melted chocolate, and vanilla with flour mixture. Continue as above, *except* bake 9 to 11 minutes.

Nutrition information per cookie: 84 calories, 1 g protein, 12 g carbohydrate, 4 g fat (1 g saturated), 4 mg cholesterol, 53 mg sodium, 32 mg potassium.

Oatmeal-Raisin Cookies

½ cup margarine *or* butter
½ cup shortening
2 cups all-purpose flour
1¾ cups packed brown sugar
2 eggs
¼ cup milk
1 teaspoon baking soda
1 teaspoon ground cinnamon
2 cups rolled oats
¾ cup raisins
½ cup chopped almonds, pecans, *or* toasted pumpkin seeds

● In a large mixer bowl beat margarine or butter and shortening with an electric mixer on medium to high speed for 30 seconds. Add *half* of the flour, the brown sugar, eggs, milk, baking soda, and cinnamon. Beat mixture till thoroughly combined. Beat or stir in the remaining flour. Stir in the oats, raisins, and almonds, pecans, or pumpkin seeds.

Drop by rounded teaspoons 2 inches apart onto an ungreased cookie sheet. Bake in a 375° oven for 8 to 10 minutes or till golden. Cool on a wire rack. Makes 66 cookies.

Nutrition information per cookie: 86 calories, 1 g protein, 12 g carbohydrate, 4 g fat (1 g saturated), 7 mg cholesterol, 34 mg sodium, 58 mg potassium.

Apple-Oatmeal Raisin Cookies
¾ cup finely shredded, peeled apple

Prepare Oatmeal-Raisin Cookies as above, *except* omit the milk. Stir shredded apple in with oats.

Nutrition information per cookie: 86 calories, 1 g protein, 12 g carbohydrate, 4 g fat (1 g saturated), 6 mg cholesterol, 34 mg sodium, 58 mg potassium.

Oatmeal-Peanut Butter Cookies
½ cup peanut butter
1 cup chopped unsalted dry roasted peanuts *or* one 6-ounce package (1 cup) semisweet chocolate pieces

Prepare Oatmeal-Raisin Cookies as above, *except* omit ground cinnamon, raisins, and chopped almonds, pecans, or pumpkin seeds. Substitute peanut butter for the shortening. Stir in peanuts or chocolate pieces with the oats.

Nutrition information per cookie: 84 calories, 2 g protein, 11 g carbohydrate, 4 g fat (1 g saturated), 7 mg cholesterol, 43 mg sodium, 67 mg potassium.

Out of Buttermilk?

If a recipe calls for buttermilk and you don't have any on hand, sour milk is a good substitute. Here's how to make it. For each cup of sour milk, place 1 tablespoon lemon juice or vinegar in a glass measuring cup. Add enough milk to make 1 cup total liquid; stir. Let the mixture stand 5 minutes before using.

HOLIDAY OPEN HOUSE

*C*apture the spirit of the holidays by inviting a few friends over for food and festivities. This colorful array of merry desserts is sure to please.

MENU

•

WHITE CHEESECAKE
(page 83)

PAINTED SOUR CREAM SUGAR COOKIES
(page 103)

CHOCOLATE-PEANUT BUTTER FUDGE
(page 90)

Menu Countdown

1 Week Ahead: Prepare and bake *Painted Sour Cream Sugar Cookies.* Seal, label, and freeze.
2 Days Ahead: Prepare *Chocolate-* *Peanut Butter Fudge;* cover and store.
1 Day Ahead: Prepare *White Cheesecake;* cover and chill. Decorate *Painted Sour Cream Sugar Cookies.* When completely dry, cover and store.

Rolled Sour Cream Sugar Cookies

To keep your cookies looking shapely, do not use 100% corn oil margarine or spread, diet, or soft-style margarine products in these cookies. The dough will be too soft to roll out.

½ **cup margarine *or* butter**
2½ **cups all-purpose flour**
1 **cup sugar**
1 **egg**
½ **cup dairy sour cream**
1 **teaspoon baking powder**
1 **teaspoon vanilla**
¼ **teaspoon baking soda**
   Dash salt
1 **teaspoon finely shredded lemon peel *or* ¼ teaspoon ground nutmeg**
   Sugar (optional)

● In a large mixer bowl beat margarine or butter with an electric mixer on medium to high speed for 30 seconds. Add about *half* of the flour, the sugar, egg, sour cream, baking powder, vanilla, baking soda, and salt. Beat till thoroughly combined. Beat or stir in remaining flour. Stir in lemon peel or nutmeg. Divide dough in half. Cover and chill for 1 to 2 hours or till easy to handle.

On a well-floured surface roll *half* of the dough at a time to ⅛ to ¼ inch thickness. Cut into desired shapes with cookie cutters. With a wide spatula, transfer cookies to an ungreased cookie sheet, placing them ½ inch apart. If desired, sprinkle lightly with additional sugar.

Bake in a 375° oven for 7 to 8 minutes or till edges are firm and bottoms are very lightly browned. Remove and cool on wire racks. Makes 48 cookies.

Nutrition information per cookie: 64 calories, 1 g protein, 9 g carbohydrate, 3 g fat (2 g saturated), 11 mg cholesterol, 32 mg sodium, 13 mg potassium.

Painted Sour Cream Sugar Cookies
2 **cups sifted powdered sugar**
½ **teaspoon vanilla**
2 **to 3 tablespoons milk**
   Food coloring

Prepare Rolled Sour Cream Sugar Cookies as above, *except* do not sprinkle with sugar before baking. In a mixing bowl combine powdered sugar, vanilla, and enough milk to make a mixture of glazing consistency. Spread the top of each cookie with some of the glaze. Allow glaze to dry completely. Using a small paintbrush, paint designs on each cookie with food coloring.

Nutrition information per cookie: 80 calories, 1 g protein, 13 g carbohydrate, 3 g fat (2 g saturated), 11 mg cholesterol, 32 mg sodium, 14 mg potassium.

RISE AND SHINE

*B*egin your day with delectable breakfast or brunch fare. Look on the next several pages to find a variety of breakfast breads such as *Sour Cream-Honey Doughnuts* and *Oatmeal Pancakes,* and egg dishes such as *Cheesy Sausage and Egg Bake* and *Wild Rice-Feta Frittata.*

Whole Wheat-Cardamom Rolls are pictured at right.

(See recipe, page 106.)

Maple Nut-Cinnamon Rolls

Fill your kitchen with the tantalizing aroma of fresh, hot, home-baked bread. (Whole Wheat-Cardamom Rolls are pictured on page 105.)

4¼ to 4¾ cups all-purpose flour
1 package active dry yeast
1¼ cups buttermilk
¼ cup sugar
¼ cup margarine *or* butter
1 teaspoon salt
2 eggs

● Combine *1½ cups* of the all-purpose flour and the yeast. Heat and stir buttermilk, sugar, margarine, and salt just till warm (120° to 130°) and margarine almost melts. Add to flour mixture; add eggs. Beat with an electric mixer on low speed 30 seconds; scrape sides of bowl constantly. Beat on high speed 3 minutes. Stir in as much of the remaining flour as you can. (Dough will be soft.) Turn out onto a lightly floured surface. Knead in enough of the remaining flour to make a moderately soft dough that is smooth and elastic (3 to 5 minutes total). Shape into a ball. Place in a greased bowl; turn once. Cover; let rise in a warm place till double (1 to 1½ hours). Punch down; divide in half. Cover; let rest 10 minutes.

6 tablespoons margarine *or* butter, softened
¾ cups chopped walnuts *or* pecans
½ cup packed brown sugar *or* sugar
2 teaspoons ground cinnamon
Maple Glaze

● Roll *half* of the dough into a 12x8-inch rectangle. Spread with *3 tablespoons* of the softened margarine. Combine walnuts, brown sugar, and cinnamon; sprinkle *half* over dough. Roll up from one of the short sides; seal edges. Slice into 8 pieces. Repeat with remaining dough, margarine, and sugar mixture. Arrange rolls, cut-side down, in a greased 13x9x2-inch baking pan. Cover and let rise till nearly double (30 to 45 minutes). Bake in a 350° oven 25 to 30 minutes. Invert onto a wire rack. Drizzle with Maple Glaze. Makes 16.

Nutrition information per serving: 309 calories, 6 g protein, 46 g carbohydrate, 12 g fat (2 g saturated), 27 mg cholesterol, 251 mg sodium, 139 mg potassium.

Maple Glaze
1 cup sifted powdered sugar
2 tablespoons maple-flavored syrup
2 to 3 teaspoons water *or* milk

In a mixing bowl stir together powdered sugar and maple-flavored syrup. Stir in enough water or milk to make a mixture of drizzling consistency.

Whole Wheat-Cardamom Rolls
2 cups whole wheat flour
2¼ to 2¾ cups all-purpose flour
1 tablespoon finely shredded lemon peel
¾ teaspoon ground cardamom

Prepare Maple Nut-Cinnamon Rolls as above, *except* substitute whole wheat flour for 2 cups of the stirred-in all-purpose flour. Stir in lemon peel with the whole wheat flour. Substitute the cardamom for the cinnamon.

Nutrition information per serving: 302 calories, 6 g protein, 45 g carbohydrate, 12 g fat (2 g saturated), 27 mg cholesterol, 251 mg sodium, 176 mg potassium.

Almond-Crunch Apricot Muffins

Apricot nectar and dried apricots add a tasty fruit flavor to these streusel-topped muffins. (Pictured on page 122.)

2 tablespoons sugar
4 teaspoons all-purpose flour
1 tablespoon margarine *or* butter
2 tablespoons chopped almonds

● Line 12 muffin cups with paper bake cups. For topping, in a mixing bowl combine sugar and the 4 teaspoons flour. Cut in margarine or butter till crumbly. Stir in almonds. Set aside.

1¾ cups all-purpose flour
⅓ cup packed brown sugar
2 teaspoons baking powder
½ teaspoon ground cinnamon
¼ teaspoon baking soda
⅛ teaspoon ground allspice

● In a mixing bowl stir together the 1¾ cups flour, the brown sugar, baking powder, cinnamon, baking soda, and allspice. Make a well in the center of the dry ingredients.

1 beaten egg
1 5½-ounce can apricot nectar *or* apple juice
⅓ cup cooking oil
¾ cup finely snipped dried apricots *or* dried apples

● Combine the egg, apricot nectar or apple juice, and cooking oil. Add egg mixture all at once to dry ingredients. Stir *just till moistened* (batter should be lumpy). Fold in dried apricots.
  Divide batter evenly among the 12 prepared muffin cups. Sprinkle the topping over the batter in each cup.

● Bake in a 400° oven for 15 to 20 minutes or till golden. Remove muffins from pans; serve warm. Makes 12 muffins.

Nutrition information per serving: 204 calories, 3 g protein, 30 g carbohydrate, 8 g fat (1 g saturated), 18 mg cholesterol, 86 mg sodium, 185 mg potassium.

The Perfect Muffin

Muffins are both quick and easy to make. And who can resist a scrumptious bite of a warm-from-the-oven muffin? By carefully following the recipe directions and these tips, you can create the perfect muffin.
● After you add the liquid ingredients to the flour mixture, stir until the dry ingredients are *just moistened*. Do not beat the batter smooth. Overmixed muffins will be peaked and smooth on top and have a tough, heavy texture with holes or tunnels.
● To check for doneness, look for golden tops. Also, a wooden toothpick inserted near the center of a muffin comes out clean when the muffins are done.
● Remove baked muffins from the pan immediately after removing from the oven. This prevents the muffin sides and bottoms from becoming soggy.
● Seal, label, and freeze leftover muffins for up to 2 months. Thaw, unwrapped, at room temperature for 1 hour. Or, heat in a 300° oven for 25 minutes or till muffins are heated through.

Blueberry-Orange Muffins

Yogurt adds a pleasant, tangy flavor to these blueberry-laden muffins.

1¾ **cups all-purpose flour**
¼ **cup sugar**
2½ **teaspoons baking powder**

● Lightly grease 12 muffin cups or line with paper bake cups; set aside. In a mixing bowl combine the flour, the ¼ cup sugar, and baking powder. Make a well in the center of the flour mixture.

1 **beaten egg**
1 **8-ounce carton orange *or* vanilla yogurt**
¼ **cup cooking oil**
1 **teaspoon finely shredded orange peel**
¾ **cup fresh *or* frozen blueberries**

● In a mixing bowl stir together the egg, yogurt, oil, and orange peel. Add all at once to the flour mixture. Stir *just till moistened* (batter should be lumpy). Fold in the fresh or frozen blueberries.

Sugar (optional)

● Divide the batter evenly among the prepared muffin cups. If desired, sprinkle tops of batter with additional sugar.

● Bake in a 400° oven about 20 minutes or till golden. Remove muffins from pans; serve warm. Makes 12 muffins.

Nutrition information per serving: 154 calories, 3 g protein, 23 g carbohydrate, 5 g fat (1 g saturated), 19 mg cholesterol, 77 mg sodium, 71 mg potassium.

Make It Easy
1 **15.2-ounce package blueberry quick bread mix**

Prepare Blueberry-Orange Muffins as above, *except* omit the flour, ¼ cup sugar, baking powder, and blueberries. Combine muffin mix with egg, yogurt, cooking oil, and orange peel. Bake as above.

Nutrition information per serving: 213 calories, 3 g protein, 30 g carbohydrate, 9 g fat (1 g saturated), 19 mg cholesterol, 173 mg sodium, 63 mg potassium.

Oatmeal Pancakes

Keep the first pancakes "hot off the griddle" by placing them on an ovenproof plate and putting the plate in a 300° oven while you cook the remaining pancakes.

1 cup milk
¾ cup quick-cooking rolled oats

● In a small saucepan heat milk till hot. Stir in oats; let stand, covered, 5 minutes.

¾ cup all-purpose flour
2 tablespoons brown sugar
2 teaspoons baking powder
¼ teaspoon salt
⅛ teaspoon baking soda

● Meanwhile, in a mixing bowl combine the flour, brown sugar, baking powder, salt, and baking soda. Stir in the oat mixture.

2 beaten eggs
1 tablespoon cooking oil

● Stir together the beaten eggs and cooking oil; add all at once to flour-oat mixture. Stir mixture *just till blended* but still slightly lumpy.

● For each pancake, pour about *¼ cup* of the batter onto a hot, lightly greased griddle or heavy skillet, and let it spread to about a 4-inch circle.

● Cook till pancakes are golden brown, turning to cook second sides when pancakes have a bubbly surface and slightly dry edges.

Strawberry-Orange Sauce *or* maple-flavored syrup

● Serve pancakes with warm Strawberry-Orange Sauce or maple-flavored syrup. Makes 8 pancakes (4 servings).

Nutrition information per serving: 354 calories, 11 g protein, 53 g carbohydrate, 11 g fat (3 g saturated), 112 mg cholesterol, 404 mg sodium, 418 mg potassium.

Strawberry-Orange Sauce
1 cup orange juice
2 teaspoons cornstarch
1 cup sliced fresh strawberries
1 tablespoon margarine *or* butter
1 tablespoon honey

In a small saucepan stir together the juice and cornstarch. Cook and stir over medium heat till thickened and bubbly. Cook and stir for 2 minutes more. Stir in the strawberries, margarine or butter, and honey, stirring till margarine melts. Makes 1½ cups.

Cream Cheese Waffles

Arrange the baked waffles in a single layer on a wire rack. Place the rack on a baking sheet and place the baking sheet in a 300° oven while remaining waffles are baking.

1¾ cups all-purpose flour
2 tablespoons brown sugar
1 tablespoon baking powder
⅛ teaspoon salt

● In a mixing bowl combine flour, brown sugar, baking powder, and salt.

1 3-ounce package cream cheese, softened
2 egg yolks
1½ cups milk
2 tablespoons cooking oil

● In another bowl stir together cream cheese and egg yolks till smooth. Stir milk and oil into the egg yolk mixture. Add egg yolk mixture to flour mixture all at once. Stir *just till combined* but still slightly lumpy.

2 egg whites

● In a mixing bowl beat egg whites till stiff peaks form (tips stand straight). Gently fold beaten egg whites into flour and egg yolk mixture, leaving a few fluffs of egg whites in the batter. *Do not overmix.*

● Pour about 1 to 1¼ cups batter onto grids of a preheated, lightly greased waffle iron. Close lid quickly; *do not open* during baking. Bake according to manufacturer's directions. When done, use a fork to lift waffle off grid.

Fresh fruit (optional)
Flavored yogurt (optional)

● Repeat with remaining batter. If desired, serve with fresh fruit and/or yogurt. Makes 4 to 6 waffles (4 to 6 servings).

Nutrition information per serving: 446 calories, 14 g protein, 54 g carbohydrate, 19 g fat (8 g saturated), 138 mg cholesterol, 428 mg sodium, 284 mg potassium.

Buttermilk-Pecan Waffles
½ cup ground pecans
¼ teaspoon baking soda
1½ cups buttermilk

Prepare Cream Cheese Waffles as above, *except* decrease flour to 1½ cups. Stir pecans and baking soda in with the flour. Substitute buttermilk for the milk.

Nutrition information per serving: 509 calories, 14 g protein, 51 g carbohydrate, 28 g fat (8 g saturated), 133 mg cholesterol, 530 mg sodium, 332 mg potassium.

Bran Waffles
½ cup whole bran cereal

Prepare Cream Cheese Waffles as above, *except* decrease flour to 1½ cups. Stir bran cereal in with flour.

Nutrition information per serving: 440 calories, 14 g protein, 54 g carbohydrate, 19 g fat (8 g saturated), 138 mg cholesterol, 485 mg sodium, 379 mg potassium.

French Toast

Create a French-toast treat by using slices of homemade Double-Swirl Apple Bread (see recipe, page 74) instead of purchased bread.

3 eggs
¾ cup milk
1 tablespoon honey
1 teaspoon vanilla
¼ teaspoon ground allspice, nutmeg, *or* cinnamon

● In a shallow bowl beat together the eggs, milk, honey, vanilla, and allspice, nutmeg, or cinnamon.

8 to 10 slices dry white, whole wheat, French, *or* Italian bread

● Dip bread into egg mixture, coating both sides. (If using French or Italian bread, let soak in egg mixture about 15 seconds on each side.)

1 tablespoon margarine, butter, *or* cooking oil

● In a skillet or on a griddle cook bread in hot margarine, butter, or oil over medium heat for 2 to 3 minutes on each side or till golden brown. Add more margarine, butter, or cooking oil as needed.

Sifted powdered sugar *or* maple-flavored syrup (optional)

● If desired, serve with powdered sugar or maple-flavored syrup. Makes 4 servings.

Nutrition information per serving: 271 calories, 11 g protein, 35 g carbohydrate, 10 g fat (3 g saturated), 164 mg cholesterol, 390 mg sodium, 184 mg potassium.

Fruity French Toast
½ cup peach, apricot, *or* strawberry preserves
¼ cup orange juice
1½ cups peeled and sliced fresh peaches, nectarines, *or* sliced strawberries

Prepare French Toast as above, *except* omit powdered sugar or maple-flavored syrup. For the sauce, combine preserves and orange juice in a small saucepan. Heat through.

To serve, top each serving with fresh fruit. Drizzle with the sauce.

Nutrition information per serving: 413 calories, 12 g protein, 71 g carbohydrate, 10 g fat (3 g saturated), 164 mg cholesterol, 395 mg sodium, 376 mg potassium.

Sour Cream-Honey Doughnuts

3 cups all-purpose flour
1 tablespoon baking powder
½ teaspoon ground cinnamon
¼ teaspoon baking soda
¼ teaspoon salt

● In a bowl stir together flour, baking powder, cinnamon, baking soda, and salt. Set aside.

2 eggs
½ cup sugar
½ cup dairy sour cream
¼ cup honey
¼ cup cooking oil, or margarine or
   butter, melted

● In another mixing bowl beat eggs about 4 minutes or till thick and lemon-colored. Beat in sugar, sour cream, honey, and oil, margarine, or butter. Stir in dry ingredients *just till combined.* Cover. Chill dough for 2 to 4 hours or till easy to handle.

Cooking oil *or* shortening for deep-fat frying

● On a lightly floured surface, roll *half* of the dough to ½-inch thickness. Cut with a floured 2½-inch doughnut cutter, rerolling as necessary. Repeat with the remaining dough.
   In a Dutch oven or deep-fat fryer heat 1½ to 2 inches cooking oil or melted shortening to 375°. Carefully fry 2 or 3 doughnuts at a time in hot fat about 2 minutes or till golden, turning once. Repeat with remaining doughnuts and doughnut holes.

Sifted powdered sugar, sugar, *or* Powdered Sugar Glaze (optional)

● If desired, shake warm doughnuts in a bag with powdered sugar or sugar. Or, drizzle with Powdered Sugar Glaze. Makes 18 doughnuts (18 servings).

Nutrition information per serving: 268 calories, 3 g protein, 26 g carbohydrate, 17 g fat (3 g saturated), 27 mg cholesterol, 100 mg sodium, 42 mg potassium.

Powdered Sugar Glaze
2 cups powdered sugar
1 teaspoon vanilla
2 to 3 tablespoons milk

In a small bowl combine the powdered sugar and vanilla. Stir in enough milk to make a mixture of glazing consistency.

Gingerbread Doughnuts
½ teaspoon ground ginger
½ cup packed brown sugar
¼ cup light molasses
1 teaspoon finely shredded lemon peel
1 tablespoon lemon juice

Prepare Sour Cream-Honey Doughnuts as above, *except* stir ginger in with the cinnamon. Substitute the brown sugar for the ½ cup sugar. Substitute molasses for the honey.
   Prepare Powdered Sugar Glaze as above, *except* omit vanilla. Stir the lemon peel and lemon juice into the powdered sugar.

Nutrition information per serving: 265 calories, 3 g protein, 25 g carbohydrate, 17 g fat (3 g saturated), 27 mg cholesterol, 103 mg sodium, 102 mg potassium.

Blueberry Coffee Cake

When fresh, sweet blueberries are spilling over on your grocer's shelves, buy a box and whip up this simple breakfast or snack cake.

1½ **cups all-purpose flour**
 1 **cup sugar**
 ¼ **teaspoon salt**
 ½ **cup margarine *or* butter**
 ⅓ **cup finely chopped pecans *or* walnuts**
 ¼ **teaspoon ground nutmeg, ground**
   cardamom, *or* ground cinnamon

● For crumb mixture, in a mixing bowl combine flour, sugar, and salt. Cut in margarine or butter till mixture resembles fine crumbs. Remove *½ cup* of the crumb mixture for topping. Stir the pecans or walnuts and nutmeg, cardamom, or cinnamon into the topping. Set aside.

½ **teaspoon baking soda**
 1 **slightly beaten egg**
 ½ **cup buttermilk *or* sour milk**
   (see tip, page 101)

● Stir the baking soda into the remaining crumb mixture. Make a well in the center of the crumb mixture. Stir together beaten egg and buttermilk or sour milk. Add egg mixture all at once to the crumb mixture. Stir *just till moistened.*

1½ **cups fresh *or* frozen blueberries**

● Spread batter into a lightly greased 9-inch round baking pan. Top with blueberries. (Do not thaw frozen blueberries.) Sprinkle reserved topping mixture over blueberries.

● Bake in a 350° oven for 40 to 45 minutes or till golden. Serve warm. Makes 8 servings.

Nutrition information per serving: 348 calories, 4 g protein, 49 g carbohydrate, 16 g fat (3 g saturated), 27 mg cholesterol, 278 mg sodium, 106 mg potassium.

Blueberry-Lemon Coffee Cake
 1 **teaspoon finely shredded lemon peel**

Prepare Blueberry Coffee Cake as above, *except* stir the lemon peel into the crumb mixture along with the baking soda.

Raspberry-Oat Coffee Cake

No kneading is needed for this yeast-leavened coffee cake—just mix and let it rise.

1 **package active dry yeast**
¼ **cup warm water (110° to 115°)**

● Soften yeast in the warm water.

½ **cup margarine *or* butter**
3½ **cups all-purpose flour**
½ **cup rolled oats**
½ **cup milk**
3 **beaten eggs**
⅓ **cup packed brown sugar**
½ **teaspoon salt**

● Meanwhile, in a mixer bowl beat the margarine or butter with an electric mixer on medium speed for 30 seconds. Add *1 cup* of the flour, the rolled oats, milk, eggs, brown sugar, salt, and the yeast mixture.
　　Beat on low speed of an electric mixer for 30 seconds, scraping sides of bowl constantly. Beat on high speed for 3 minutes. Beat or stir in the remaining flour till well blended.

½ **cup seedless raspberry preserves**
¼ **cup chopped almonds**

● Grease two 8-inch round baking pans or one 13x9x2-inch baking pan. Spread *half* of the dough evenly in prepared pans.
　　Combine the preserves and the almonds. Spoon preserves mixture evenly over dough in pans. Spoon remaining dough in small mounds on top of the preserves mixture, covering as much of the preserves as possible.

¼ **cup all-purpose flour**
¼ **cup sugar**
¼ **cup rolled oats**
½ **teaspoon ground cinnamon**
3 **tablespoons margarine *or* butter**

● For topping, in a mixing bowl combine the ¼ cup flour, the sugar, oats, and cinnamon. Cut in the margarine or butter to make a crumb mixture. Sprinkle topping evenly over top layer of dough. Cover and let rise in a warm place till nearly double (30 to 40 minutes).

Powdered Sugar Icing

● Bake in a 350° oven for 30 to 35 minutes for the 8-inch round pans or 35 to 40 minutes for the 13x9x2-inch pan. Cool slightly.
　　Drizzle with Powdered Sugar Icing. Serve warm. Makes 12 to 16 servings.

Nutrition information per serving: 297 calories, 6 g protein, 45 g carbohydrate, 11 g fat (2 g saturated), 41 mg cholesterol, 179 mg sodium, 122 mg potassium.

Powdered Sugar Icing
¾ **cup sifted powdered sugar**
½ **teaspoon vanilla**
2 **to 3 teaspoons milk**

In a mixing bowl stir together the powdered sugar and vanilla. Stir in enough of the milk to make an icing of drizzling consistency.

Orange-Hazelnut Braid

2¾ to 3¼ cups all-purpose flour
1 package active dry yeast
⅔ cup milk
⅓ cup sugar
¼ cup margarine *or* butter
½ teaspoon salt
1 egg
1 teaspoon finely shredded orange peel

● In a mixer bowl combine *1¼ cups* of the flour and the yeast. In a saucepan heat milk, sugar, margarine or butter, and salt just till warm (120° to 130°) and margarine is almost melted, stirring constantly. Add to flour mixture. Add egg. Beat with an electric mixer on low speed for 30 seconds, scraping sides of bowl constantly. Beat on high speed for 3 minutes. Using a wooden spoon, stir in the orange peel and as much of the remaining flour as you can.

Turn dough out onto a lightly floured surface. Knead in enough of the remaining flour to make a moderately stiff dough that is smooth and elastic (6 to 8 minutes total). Shape into a ball. Place in a greased bowl; turn once to grease surface of dough. Cover; let rise in a warm place till double (1 to 1¼ hours).

1 cup hazelnuts *or* pecans, ground
⅔ cup sifted powdered sugar
¼ cup margarine *or* butter, softened

● For filling, in a mixing bowl stir ground nuts and powdered sugar into softened margarine or butter. Set mixture aside.

1 cup sifted powdered sugar
3 to 4 teaspoons of milk

● Punch dough down. Cover; let rest 10 minutes. On a lightly floured surface, roll dough into an 18x9-inch rectangle. Spread the filling over *half* of the dough along a long side. Fold remaining half of dough over filling. Cut the dough lengthwise into 4 (about 18x1¼-inch) strips. Twist each strip 6 to 8 times.

On a large greased baking sheet, hold the end of a strip in the center of the baking sheet. Wrap the strip around its end, forming a coil. Brush end with water. Pinch the end of a second strip to the end of the first strip; continue coiling dough. Repeat with remaining strips, tucking the end of the last strip underneath the coil.

Cover and let rise till nearly double in size (about 45 minutes). Bake in a 375° oven for 25 to 30 minutes or till bread sounds hollow when you tap the top with your fingers (if necessary, loosely cover with foil the last 10 minutes of baking to prevent overbrowning). *Immediately* remove bread from pan. Cool on a wire rack.

Stir together powdered sugar and enough milk to make a glaze of drizzling consistency. Drizzle over coffee cake. Serves 10 to 12.

Nutrition information per serving: 388 calories, 7 g protein, 52 g carbohydrate, 18 g fat (3 g saturated), 23 mg cholesterol, 231 mg sodium, 142 mg potassium.

Apple-Cinnamon Oatmeal

Oats were brought to North America around 1602, but it was many years before they were considered a staple food. Oats were prepared most often as "hot porridge" or oatmeal.

3 cups apple juice
1½ cups regular rolled oats
½ cup shredded peeled apple
¼ cup raisins, mixed dried fruit bits, snipped dried apricots, *or* dried tart red cherries
¼ teaspoon salt
¼ teaspoon apple pie spice *or* ground cinnamon

● In a large saucepan stir together the apple juice, oats, apple, dried fruit, salt, and apple pie spice or cinnamon. Bring mixture to boiling; reduce heat. Simmer, uncovered, for 5 minutes, stirring occasionally. Cover; remove mixture from heat. Let stand about 5 minutes before serving or till desired consistency is reached.

4 teaspoons brown sugar
Milk

● Spoon into 4 serving bowls. Sprinkle *each* serving with *1 teaspoon* of the brown sugar. Pass the milk. Makes 4 servings.

Nutrition information per serving: 271 calories, 5 g protein, 59 g carbohydrate, 2 g fat (0 g saturated), 0 mg cholesterol, 144 mg sodium, 445 mg potassium.

Mandarin-Orange Oatmeal
3 cups water
⅛ teaspoon ground ginger
1 11-ounce can mandarin orange sections, drained

Prepare Apple-Cinnamon Oatmeal as above, *except* omit the apple juice, apple, and dried fruit. Combine the water and ginger with the oats, salt, and apple pie spice or cinnamon. After simmering this mixture for 5 minutes, stir in the orange sections. Serve as above.

Nutrition information per serving: 173 calories, 5 g protein, 35 g carbohydrate, 2 g fat (0 g saturated), 0 mg cholesterol, 140 mg sodium, 173 mg potassium.

Chocolate Oatmeal
3 cups water
¼ cup chocolate-flavored syrup
4 teaspoons sugar (optional)
4 teaspoons miniature semi-sweet chocolate pieces (optional)

Prepare Apple-Cinnamon Oatmeal as above, *except* omit the apple juice, apple, dried fruit, apple pie spice or cinnamon, and brown sugar. Combine the water and chocolate-flavored syrup with the oats and salt. Cook as above. If desired, sprinkle each serving with sugar and chocolate pieces.

Nutrition information per serving: 159 calories, 5 g protein, 31 g carbohydrate, 2 g fat (0 g saturated), 0 mg cholesterol, 150 mg sodium, 149 mg potassium.

Cheesy Sausage and Egg Bake

Brighten your brunch table with this scrambled egg casserole. Besides being eye-catching, it's easy on the host, too. You can make it the day before and store it in the refrigerator.

½ **pound bulk pork sausage** *or*
    turkey breakfast sausage
1 **2½-ounce jar sliced mushrooms,**
    drained

● In a large skillet cook sausage till no longer pink. Drain off fat. Stir in mushrooms. Transfer to a mixing bowl. Set aside. Wash the skillet.

1 **tablespoon margarine** *or* **butter**
2 **tablespoons all-purpose flour**
    Dash pepper
1 **cup milk**
¾ **cup shredded American cheese**
    (3 ounces)

● Meanwhile, for the sauce, in a small saucepan melt margarine or butter. Stir in flour and a dash of pepper. Add milk all at once. Cook and stir over medium heat till thickened and bubbly. Cook and stir for 1 minute more. Stir in cheese till melted. Remove from heat. Set aside.

10 **eggs**
2 **tablespoons grated Parmesan cheese**
¼ **teaspoon pepper**
1 **4-ounce can diced green chili**
    peppers, drained (optional)

● In a mixing bowl beat together eggs, Parmesan cheese, and the ¼ teaspoon pepper. If desired, stir in chili peppers. Set aside.

1 **tablespoon margarine** *or* **butter**

● In the large skillet melt margarine or butter. Add the egg mixture. Cook over medium heat without stirring till mixture begins to set on the bottom and around the edge. Using a large spoon or spatula lift and fold partially cooked eggs so uncooked portion flows underneath. Continue cooking over medium heat till eggs are cooked throughout but are still glossy and moist. Remove eggs from heat immediately.

● Transfer *half* of the eggs into a 10x6x2-inch baking dish. Top with sausage-mushroom mixture. Pour *half* of the cheese sauce atop. Layer remaining eggs atop cheese sauce. Pour remaining cheese sauce evenly over all.

1 **tomato, chopped**
¼ **cup sliced green onion**

● Cover and bake in a 350° oven about 25 minutes or till heated through. Top with tomato and green onion. Makes 6 servings.

Nutrition information per serving: 349 calories, 21 g protein, 6 g carbohydrate, 26 g fat (10 g saturated), 395 mg cholesterol, 787 mg sodium, 302 mg potassium.

Make-Ahead Directions: Prepare the Cheesy Sausage and Egg Bake as above, *except* after assembling, cover and chill for up to 24 hours. Cover and bake in a 350° oven for 40 to 45 minutes or till heated through. Serve as above.

119

Wild Rice and Feta Frittata

If your skillet has a plastic or wooden handle, you still can use it under the broiler if you wrap the handle well with foil.

6 eggs
⅛ teaspoon salt
⅛ teaspoon pepper
½ cup cooked wild rice

● In a mixing bowl beat the eggs, salt, and pepper; stir in the rice. Set aside.

¼ cup sliced green onion
1 tablespoon margarine *or* butter
½ cup finely crumbled feta cheese *or* blue cheese (2 ounces)

● In a 10-inch broilerproof skillet cook the ¼ cup green onion in margarine or butter till tender. Pour the egg mixture into the skillet over the onion mixture. Sprinkle with the feta or blue cheese.

3 thinly sliced sweet red pepper rings

● Cook over medium heat. As mixture sets, run a spatula around edge of skillet, lifting egg mixture to allow uncooked portions to flow underneath. Continue cooking and lifting edges till egg mixture is almost set (surface will be moist). Arrange red pepper rings atop eggs.

Sliced green onions (optional)

● Place the broilerproof skillet under the broiler 4 to 5 inches from the heat. Broil 1 to 2 minutes or till top is just set. If desired, garnish with additional green onions. Cut into wedges to serve. Makes 3 servings.

Nutrition information per serving: 268 calories, 17 g protein, 9 g carbohydrate, 18 g fat (7 g saturated), 443 mg cholesterol, 468 mg sodium, 208 mg potassium.

As the eggs begin to set, run a wide spatula around the edge of the skillet and lift the eggs. Lifting the eggs allows the uncooked portion to flow underneath and cook. The top will finish cooking under the broiler.

Gazpacho-Topped Omelet

Omelets are so quick to fix that you can easily serve three or four people this brunch or main-dish omelet. Just increase the recipe according to the number of people you're serving.

¾ **cup chopped tomato**
¼ **cup chopped zucchini *or* cucumber**
1 **tablespoon sliced green onion**
  Dash bottled hot pepper sauce

● For gazpacho sauce, in a small saucepan combine tomato, zucchini or cucumber, green onion, and hot pepper sauce. Cook, covered, for 5 minutes over medium heat. Keep warm.

2 **eggs**
2 **tablespoons water**
⅛ **teaspoon salt**
  Dash pepper
1 **teaspoon snipped parsley (optional)**
¼ **teaspoon dried oregano *or* basil, crushed (optional)**

● Meanwhile, in a mixing bowl combine the eggs, water, salt, and pepper. If desired, stir in parsley and oregano or basil. Using a fork, beat till combined but not frothy.

2 **teaspoons margarine *or* butter**

● In an 8- or 10-inch skillet with flared sides, heat margarine or butter till a drop of water sizzles. Lift and tilt the pan to coat the sides.

● Add egg mixture to the skillet; cook over medium heat. As eggs set, run a spatula around the edge of the skillet, lifting eggs and letting the uncooked portion flow underneath. When eggs are set but still shiny, remove from heat.

½ **cup shredded cheddar cheese, Monterey Jack cheese, or Monterey Jack cheese with jalapeño peppers**

● Sprinkle the cheese on *half* of the omelet; fold omelet in half. Transfer to a warm serving plate; top with sauce. Makes 1 serving.

Nutrition information per serving: 481 calories, 28 g protein, 10 g carbohydrate, 37 g fat (17 g saturated), 486 mg cholesterol, 844 mg sodium, 579 mg potassium.

WEEKEND BRUNCH

Celebrate the week-
end by preparing a spectacular, yet casual,
brunch. And if the weather's warm and
sunny, go alfresco.

MENU

•

HAM-ASPARAGUS STRATA
(page 123)

ALMOND-CRUNCH APRICOT MUFFINS
(page 107)

FRESH FRUIT

Menu Countdown

4 to 26 Hours Ahead: Prepare *Ham-Asparagus Strata;* cover and chill.
1¼ Hours Ahead: Bake *Ham-*

Asparagus Strata.
35 Minutes Ahead: Prepare *Almond-Crunch Apricot Muffins.*
20 Minutes Ahead: Bake *Almond-Crunch Apricot Muffins.*

Ham-Asparagus Strata

Strata is a good menu choice for brunch because it's made ahead and chilled before baking. But if you don't want to wait, we've included directions so you can bake it immediately.

4 English muffins, torn or cut into bite-sized pieces
6 ounces fully-cooked ham, cubed (about 1 cup)
½ of a 10-ounce package frozen cut asparagus *or* frozen cut broccoli, thawed and well-drained
6 1-ounce slices process Swiss cheese, torn

● In a greased 8x8x2-inch baking dish layer *half* of the English muffin pieces. Top with the ham, asparagus or broccoli, and cheese. Top with the remaining English muffin pieces.

4 beaten eggs
1¾ cups milk
½ cup dairy sour cream
2 tablespoons finely chopped onion
1 tablespoon Dijon-style *or* prepared mustard
¼ teaspoon caraway seed
⅛ teaspoon pepper

● In a mixing bowl combine the beaten eggs, milk, sour cream, onion, mustard, caraway seed, and pepper. Pour over the layers in dish. Cover and chill in the refrigerator for 2 to 24 hours.

● Bake, uncovered, in a 325° oven for 50 to 55 minutes or till a knife inserted near the center comes out clean. Let stand for 5 to 10 minutes before serving. Makes 6 servings.

Nutrition information per serving: 371 calories, 26 g protein, 25 g carbohydrate, 19 g fat (10 g saturated), 196 mg cholesterol, 1,181 mg sodium, 607 mg potassium.

Make It Easy
5 cups soft bread cubes (7 to 8 slices)

Prepare Ham-Asparagus Strata as above, *except* omit the English muffins and reduce the milk to 1½ cups. Continue as above, *except* do not chill.

Bake in a 325° oven about 65 minutes or till a knife inserted near the center comes out clean. Let stand 5 to 10 minutes before serving.

Scrambled Eggs and New Potatoes

Sometimes known as Farmer's Breakfast, this egg, meat, and potato combination makes a hearty breakfast, lunch, or dinner.

1 cup chopped tiny new potatoes
¼ cup chopped green onions *or* onion
¼ cup chopped green *or* sweet red pepper
3 tablespoons margarine *or* butter

● In a large nonstick or well-seasoned skillet cook potatoes, green onions or onion, and green or sweet red pepper in margarine or butter over medium heat for 8 to 10 minutes or till tender, stirring often.

4 ounces thinly sliced Polish sausage
6 eggs
2 tablespoons milk
½ teaspoon dried marjoram *or* basil, crushed
¼ teaspoon pepper

● Meanwhile, halve the sausage slices. Beat together the eggs, milk, marjoram or basil, and pepper. Stir in the sausage. Pour the egg mixture over the potato mixture.

¼ cup finely shredded cheddar, American, *or* Swiss cheese (1 ounce)

● Cook, without stirring, till mixture begins to set on the bottom and around the edge. Using a large spoon or spatula, lift and fold partially cooked egg mixture so uncooked portion flows underneath. Continue cooking about 3 to 4 minutes or till eggs are cooked throughout but still glossy and moist. Sprinkle the cheese atop egg mixture. Makes 4 servings.

Nutrition information per serving: 364 calories, 17 g protein, 14 g carbohydrate, 27 g fat (9 g saturated), 348 mg cholesterol, 492 mg sodium, 389 mg potassium.

Make It Easy
2 cups loose-pack frozen hash brown potatoes with onion and peppers

Prepare Scrambled Eggs and New Potatoes as above, *except* omit the potatoes, green onions or onion, and green or sweet red pepper. Cook the frozen potatoes in the margarine or butter over medium heat about 10 minutes or till tender, stirring often.

Nutrition information per serving: 465 calories, 18 g protein, 22 g carbohydrate, 35 g fat (12 g saturated), 348 mg cholesterol, 511 mg sodium, 494 mg potassium.

Index

A-B

Keep track of your daily nutrition needs by using the information we provide at the end of each recipe. We've analyzed the nutritional content of each recipe serving for you. When a recipe gives an ingredient substitution, we used the first choice in the analysis. If it makes a range of servings (such as 4 to 6), we used the smallest number. Ingredients listed as optional weren't included in the calculations.

C

T-Z

Tips

COMFORT FOOD
Editor: Jennifer Darling
Graphic Designer: Mick Schnepf
Project Manager: Jennifer Speer Ramundt

Associate Department Editor: Sandra Granseth
Associate Art Director: Linda Ford Vermie
Publishing Systems Text Processor: Paula Forest
Test Kitchen Product Supervisor: Colleen Weeden
Food Stylists: Lynn Blanchard, Carol Grones (pages 4–5), Janet Herwig
Photographers: Dennis Becker, Mike Dieter (cover), M. Jensen Photography

BETTER HOMES AND GARDENS® BOOKS
An Imprint of Meredith® Books
Vice President and Editorial Director: Elizabeth P. Rice
Food and Family Life Editor: Sharyl Heiken
Art Director: Ernest Shelton
Managing Editor: David A. Kirchner
Art Production Director: John Berg
Test Kitchen Director: Sharon Stilwell

President, Book Group: Joseph J. Ward
Vice President, Retail Marketing: Jamie L. Martin
Vice President, Book Clubs: Richard L. Rundall